Worceste Countryside

Cataloguing in Publication Data is available from the British Library

ISBN 1-872454-03-8

Copyright: The author and publisher are pleased for owners wishing to minimise book damage to photocopy single pages for their personal outdoor use. In all other respects no part or section whole or incomplete of this book may be reproduced transmitted or stored in any system or format without the written permission of the publisher.

Maps: All maps reproduced in this book are based upon the 1988 Ordnance Survey 1:50,000 Landranger Series maps with permission of the Controller of Her Majesty's Stationary Office. © Crown Copyright.

Publisher: Minton & Minton, Greylands, Bicton Pool, Kingsland, Nr. Leominster, Herefordshire HR6 9PR. Tel: Yarpole (0568 85) 338.

Typesetter: Myst Limited, Weobley, Herefordshire.
Typeface: Souvenir 10/11 point, headings 16 point.

Printer: Lambert & Son, Station Road, Settle, North Yorkshire.

Photography: David Minton.

Vignettes: S. G. Minton, Leominster.

Cover: The cover picture is an oil painting of the countryside near Frith Common in the Teme Valley near Eardiston. Painted by Ian Grimshaw, a professional landscape artist and portraitist, it shows the west Worcestershire landscape at its very best.

Acknowledgements: I am grateful to the following friends and colleagues for help in compiling this book and thank them for their practical support and encouragement.
Julia Ingram, whose help in typing the manuscript and commenting on the text was invaluable.
Ian Grimshaw who painted the superb cover.
Stuart Dodd, for his painstaking production of the site maps.
Harry Green of the WNCT, for information about Trust sites and helpful comments on the text.
Robert Wilkins and Ann Lloyd of H & W Countryside Service for all their advice and information.
Many other people have given help during the book's preparation including Nick Riding and Dave Entwhistle of HWCC, David Hollis, who provided the back cover photograph; Peter Boland and Colin Reid of Dudley MBC for information about Wychbury Hill and local geology respectively; The Woodland Trust; and many others who have provided useful information.
My thanks to all
Brett Westwood

Abbreviations

BC   Butterfly Conservation
BCC   Birmingham City Council
BTO   British Trust for Ornithology
FC   Forestry Commission
GR   Grid Reference
HWCC   Hereford & Worcester County Council
HWCS   Hereford & Worcester Countryside Service
MHDC   Malvern Hills District Council
MRW   Midland Red West
OSL   Ordnance Survey Landranger Map
OSP   Ordnance Survey Pathfinder Map
RBC   Redditch Borough Council
WDC   Wychavon District Council
WFDC   Wyre Forest District Council
WMBC   West Midlands Bird Club
WNCT   Worcestershire Nature Conservation Trust

Note: The letters SO and SP before grid references refer to the national
100 Kilometre squares - most of Worcestershire lies within square SO

KEY
Motorway
River
P Parking
A roads
B roads
Church
Railway

Note: The publisher and author wish to point out that while every effort
has been made to ensure accuracy they cannot be held responsible for location errors or consequences arising from location errors.

Contents

Foreword

by
Kate Ashbrook
General Secretary, Open Spaces Society

We all need the freedom to wander harmlessly in the countryside without fear of challenge. But where can we go? The Ordnance Survey maps show public paths – which may be illegally cropped, blocked or ploughed – but we cannot legally wander from them.

Brett Westwood's guide to the Worcestershire countryside takes us to those undiscovered and forgotten places, mostly not delineated on OS maps, where we can roam off the paths. These spots may be tiny, such as Ashmoor Common on the Severn, or extensive and well known, like the Clent Hills; they may be in deepest countryside or on the West Midlands conurbation's doorstep.

When so much countryside remains forbidden, it is a joy to find a guide to freedom. Worcestershire is richly varied, and Brett leads us to hilltops, woodlands, canalsides and orchards. All are places where we can escape to enjoy the flora fauna, geology and history which he knowledgeably describes. But there are others where we can't go: Brett identifies Hagley Park as one place which has no right of access.

But there is hope for the owner was, until recently, a Countryside Commissioner, and the Commission is pledged to improving access. Perhaps by the time this book is reprinted, Brett can include Hagley Park in Worcestershire's access sites.

Many of the sites are common land which, despite its name, is not publicly owned, with no automatic right of access, although people have wandered there for centuries. In 1987 the government promised a new law for commons to make that access legal, but it has so far not kept that promise.

The Open Spaces Society is leading the campaign for the new law which will give us all the right to roam, subject to common-sense restrictions, on commons in Worcestershire and elsewhere. Meanwhile, use this book to find some of Worcestershire's secret commons.

Introduction

The subject of this book no longer exists. When the counties of Worcester-shire and Herefordshire were merged under the Local Government Act of 1972, both lost their identity, on paper at least. This experiment, designed for administrative expediency, has proved singularly unpopular with residents of both shires. It is also a hindrance to lovers of the countryside since the old boundaries are no longer shown on modern maps. However, this may be adios and not goodbye for moves are afoot to re-establish the two counties. Needless to say, this book ignores the new super-county and concentrates on the beautiful countryside of Worcestershire.

For all its closeness to Birmingham and the Black Country, which have expanded outwards to meet it, Worcestershire is a secretive place. Millions pass through the county each year along the M5 motorway en route for the delights of the south-west or the north without giving it a second glance. They are missing what residents already enjoy; the grandeur of the Malvern Hills, the scenery of the Severn and Teme and the orchards of the Vale of Evesham. And, amongst these well-known places are others, seldom visited except by locals. They include a wealth of ancient woodland, sandy heaths and streamside meadows, the vast expanse of the Wyre Forest and the bosky birchwoods of Kingsford. True, there are no beaches or even much water to speak of, and hardened ramblers will find few challenges on even the Malverns, but the county's charms are far more subtle. They are not easy to package and therein lies Worcestershire's attraction - it must be sampled, like a good wine, little and often.

But first, it is best to say what this book is not. It is not a step-by-step, stile-by-stile guide to public footpaths. With over four miles of footpath for every square mile of its surface, Worcestershire is probably the most accessible English county. Linear routes abound so that any competent map-reader can plan enough customised walks for his or her family and friends to last a lifetime. The disadvantage of footpaths is that they offer a tantalising cross-section of the landscape without allowing you to get into it. Even the excellent Regional Routes such as the Worcestershire Way cannot compensate completely for the freedom to wander at large over a wider area.

So, the sites included here are chunks of accessible countryside, all of which are explorable to a greater or lesser extent. They range from small commons of a few acres to large Country Parks owned and managed by local authorities. Some will suit the active visitor intent on riding, jogging or sailing; others are secluded spots where you can picnic in peace or get away from it all. Most sites are suitable for family outings, and a few require a spirit of adventure. All the large well-known places are included because although many readers will be aware of them, they have vital amenities such as toilets and refreshments. In addition they also offer the best opportunity to wheelchair users or less mobile visitors to get into the countryside and are invaluable for that reason alone.

If this book has a purpose at all, it is to encourage more people to explore more of Worcestershire. Getting to know the countryside has never been more important. The threats to the county are increasing with the need for more roads and more housing. In the years since World War II, the county has lost 90% of its marshes, 90% of flower-rich meadows, 30% of woodland, thousands of small ponds and most of its heathland. Reeled off like that, the figures lose their impact, but represent a devastating blow to the fabric of the countryside. However advertisers portray an England of lush landscapes where cattle graze by limpid rivers, the truth is starker. Hedges are still being ripped out at an alarming rate, old woods are still being replaced by conifer plantations and those green "meadows " are likely to be rye-grass monocultures.

The sites in this book are unrepresentative of most of Worcestershire in that they are often managed sympathetically by organisations and private owners who care for them. There are a host of other places to explore, to enjoy and to protect.

Two areas which have suffered in particular and which deserve more explanation are woods and commons.

Worcestershire Woods: Woods feature highly in the site accounts and need an introduction since each wood has an individual character shaped by its history. There are also a number of woodland words used in the text which need explaining more fully.

About 8% of the county is wooded, above the national average of 6%, though the distribution is variable. In the north-west, there are many surviving woods on steep or uneven ground - 60% of Worcestershire woods are found here between the Severn and the Teme. In the south-east, the Vale of Evesham has few trees - these were cleared in pre-Roman times to expose the light, fertile soils for agriculture.

Five thousand years ago, the county was blanketed by "wildwood", the original forest which colonised England following the last great Ice-Age. At that time a squirrel could travel from Lickey to Malvern without touching the ground. These arboreal (and hypothetical!) feats were ended by the stone axes of the Neolithic peoples who felled large areas of woodland to create villages and their surrounding farmland. River valleys were cleared first in recognition of their alluvial deposits and chains of meadows along the Severn and Avon are recorded in the Domesday Survey of 1086. At this time at least 25% of the county was still wooded.

Medieval woodland was very different in character to the woods we see

3

today in that it was managed to suit the needs of the local community. Woods were coppiced by villagers to produce timber and underwood: many woods in the county are still known as coppices or "coppy-pieces". Management depended on the habit of deciduous trees of re-growing even when cut down. New stems sprout from the stump or "stool" and the tree's life is prolonged. the resulting growth of "poles" could be used for fencing (hurdles), besom-making or in house construction as wattle-and-daub. By coppicing trees in this way on a cycle of say 15 years, villagers could guarantee a continuous supply of even-aged wood. Not all trees were felled - some were retained to provide timber for house-building. Worcestershire's "black-and-white" Tudor houses, some with huge curved cruck-frames, are a product of such management. The large trees were grown over coppice to form a "coppice-with-standards" system, now reinstated in WNCT woods to benefit wildlife.

Where livestock was grazed in woods, coppicing was obviously out of the question, so trees were pollarded, that is coppiced about ten feet above the ground so that cattle could not reach them. Pollard willows are still a feature of many county river banks.

Many Worcestershire woodlands fell within the purlieu of Royal Forests, vast hunting grounds for Plantagenet and Tudor monarchs. The advent of the Black Country iron foundries and the salt industry of Droitwich made increasing demands on the woods, and, following disafforestation in the early 17th century, they began to dwindle. Coppicing virtually ceased as a commercial concern early this century, though it persisted until the 1930s in the Wyre Forest. As a result, many woods became overgrown and neglected, poor in wildlife and inhospitable to walkers. You can see excellent examples of "before and after" management at Nunnery Wood next to County Hall, Worcester.

You will find several references to "ancient" woodland in the site accounts. The word "ancient" is not used lightly, but has a precise meaning to historians and conservationists, describing woods which have been under trees continuously since at least 1600 (and by implication a great deal earlier). Some ancient woods have since been re-planted but still retain their fabric of wildlife even though the old trees have gone. Trench Wood and Uffmoor Wood are good examples, each with its flora and fauna largely intact. Over half the county's woodland is on ancient sites, distinguished by certain features. Sylvan detectives should look for irregular outlines, boundary ditches (to keep out cattle), and trees such as wild service and small-leaved lime. Ancient woods are often on steep slopes where the harrow could not reach; Perry Wood in Worcester city is a fine example.

Modern plantations are abundant, but with practice you will soon pick out their geometrical precision, the alien trees and poor ground flora. You will need to observe a new and isolated plantation for up to a century before the first bluebells arrive by natural means. Hopeful schoolchildren planting saplings en masse may be green fodder for local press reports, but are contributing little to the short-term environment. Conifers have increased in the county either as new plantings or over existing broad-leaves. The Forestry Commission is now less destructive in its approach to ancient woodland, but private companies have wrought chaos in some areas, the Suckley Hills for instance, where yews were poisoned with petrol and old limes ripped out to make way for spruce and fir.

New woods are still being created in Worcestershire. A few are appearing naturally by rivers and desiccated ponds where alders are replaced by oaks and sycamores. Most are on farmland, planted as amenity woods or for cropping and shelter-belts. Not all are of native trees and it will be centuries before they resemble the ancient woods that are such a feature of the county today.

Commons: The term 'common land' is subject to a great deal of confusion. We are all familiar with our local common; often it is scrub or grassland, unfenced, unkempt and unowned - after all isn't that what 'common' means, open to everyone?

Sadly, it doesn't. Around 80% of our commons are privately owned with access limited to rights of way, unless you are a commoner with other registered rights. Other commons are owned by local authorities, are accessible by Act of Parliament or have no registered owner. To understand how ownership affects access, we need to examine the history of common land.

In anglo-Saxon England the common people grazed cattle, tilled soil and gathered fuel on pockets of land between the manorial estates of their lords. They did not own the land, but received rights of common over it. Many of these rights survive with existing commons and included estovers (the right to take wood or bracken), pasture (right to graze livestock), pescary (the right to fish) and turbary (the right to take turf for fuel or roofing). Some commoners exercised rights of pannage, the grazing of pigs on acorns, a right that persists at Castlemorton Common.

This system was disrupted by the advent of the Norman feudal laws under which newly-created lords won land and enclosed it by the Statute of Merton in 1235. The resulting enclosures left the commoners with less land than before, generally of poorer quality.

However the real blow came in the 18th century when much of Worcestershire was enclosed between 1761 and 1820 by Act of Parliament. The Enclosures Acts divided common and waste land into a grid of fields, the so-called "planned" countryside. You can see excellent examples of this from the Malverns where the straight hedgelines to the east contrast sharply with the sinuous fields of Herefordshire to the west. The lords who passed the Acts had a vested interest in enclosing the land - they and their peers owned most of it! Thus the remaining commons were considerably reduced and the destruction continues to this day. Few modern commons reflect their original purpose-agriculture for commoners - most are now valuable for recreation and as wildlife sites.

5

County Councils are now required to keep a register of common land in which all rights of common are listed pertaining to the land concerned. You can inspect the Worcestershire register at County Hall, Worcester. Unfortunately, the register is double-edged - one commoner can prevent a landowner from enclosing the common but he or she can also sell rights to the owner thus removing any obstacle to fencing or development. The results are that private commons are disappearing.

The legal status of commons is a complex affair, but, broadly speaking, there are six types.

Private commons are owned by individuals or companies. Commoners have rights over them and they are usually crossed by rights of way. To stray off these paths is a trespass, but in practice you will rarely be challenged.

Section 9 commons have no known owner under the Commons Registration Act 1965 and are therefore open to encroachment by neighbouring landowners. Some are now under the guardianship of the Open Spaces Society who defend the rights of the public to enjoy the land. In law they are cared for by local authorities who permit walkers to use them while maintaining the rights of commoners. Hartlebury Common and Purshull Green are examples of section commons.

Regulated commons are under the stewardship of parish or district councils and you may walk freely over them. Monkwood Green is a good example of a regulated common.

Commons in trust are those held in trust by local authority appointees who manage them for specific purposes, for example their wildlife interest.

National Trust commons are generally large, open areas with access throughout to the general public. Commoners' rights are maintained. The Clent Hills are excellent examples of this type of common.

Act of Parliament commons were created to ensure the continuance of large areas of public recreation and were a direct result of pressure brought by the Commons Preservation Society, now the Open Spaces Society. All offer automatic rights of access and many have off-road parking. The Malvern Hills are fine examples of such commons.

Walking over common land is a pleasure which we should not take lightly. These are some of our best pieces of countryside with a fascinating history. They depend on regular use by members of the public. If you would like to know more about them, read the excellent introductory chapter by Dr. Brenda Swan in the Herefordshire book in this series or support them practically by joining the Open Spaces Society - commons need friends.

Using the Book

Worcestershire is a small, but remarkably diverse county. In a car, you can travel its length or breadth within an hour, but the landscape changes rapidly as you do so.

Dividing the county into manageable and, at the same time, explorable chunks has proved very difficult, so I have decided to throw logic to the winds and invent five areas, each with a variety of habitats and interest. These sections are; The Northern Hills; Western Woods & Valleys; A Ring Around Worcester; Southern Hills & Commons and The Eastern Farmlands. Some sites sit uncomfortably within these categories, but the broadly geographical divisions should help you when estimating travelling time and assessing topography. Inevitably there are areas which offer better access than others, for example the Malvern Hills. By comparison the east of the county, being lush and fertile, is largely agricultural land with few open spaces.

There are three stages to locating the sites. The first is the county sketchmap at the back of the book which shows the approximate location of each place together with its page number. The second stage is the map which appears at the head of each site description and the third the use of a more detailed O/S map for route-finding.

The location sketchmaps: Each site is portrayed on a small map designed to illustrate its position relative to towns, main roads, rivers etc. If sites are close to each other, they are shown on the same map and have consecutive descriptions within the text. Only certain features are shown, usually woods, rivers, railway lines and parking places; if you need to know details such as contour lines or the limits of common land, you should refer to the O/S pathfinder maps.

Suggested parking places are marked and are usually well-established. At some sites, for example the Malverns, parking places are legion and therefore only a selection is included.

If you use the sketchmaps in conjunction with O/S maps, you should find every site mentioned without difficulty.

Ordnance Survey Maps: The quality and ease of use of modern O/S maps makes them indispensable to any Worcestershire explorer. Two types of map are published covering the county, the Landranger and Pathfinder series. The 1:50,000 Landrangers are identified by their pink covers. Three sheets take in the county, numbers 138 (Kidderminster and the Wyre Forest), 139 (Birmingham) and 150 (Worcester and the Malverns). Rights of way are shown on these as red dashes.

7

You will need rather more of the excellent 1:25000 Pathfinder series, but they are invaluable for detailed investigations. Not only do they show all rights of way (as green dashes) but also include individual field boundaries to enable you to work out exact routes. They are, of course, no substitute for properly signposted paths and cannot keep pace with the creation of larger fields or the re-routing of paths by local authorities. In all there are 18 Pathfinders covering Worcestershire and all are worth purchasing.

The sheet numbers of the appropriate Landranger and Pathfinder maps are given at the head of each site together with a Grid Reference (GR) for suggested access points. Full details of how to take a grid reference are given on O/S maps. The only difference in this book is that the three eastings figures are separated from the northings by an oblique stroke for ease of interpretation.

Parking: There are constant references to parking places and access for drivers throughout the text. It is conventional in books such as this to bemoan the advent of the car and to recommend that you use public transport. If only you could! Many of the locations are well away from bus or train routes, so that the best means of reaching them is on foot or by car. However, basic public transport information is given for relevant sites. Parking places are therefore indicated where appropriate on all sketchmaps. For many sites there is parking only in adjoining roads or lanes. If you park in such a place, please remember to avoid blocking gateways and field entrances - in my experience a rural Parkinson's Law operates to ensure that as soon as you have blocked a gate, a farmer will want to get into the field!

Remember also that agricultural vehicles are not always built with narrow lanes in mind, so please consider them when you are parking.

The Sites: At the head of each site description is a brief summary of its location, access and features. This heading also includes notes on its steepness, muddiness, states of paths and suitability for wheelchairs. If a site is particularly difficult to get around, for example in bad weather, such details are amplified in the text. I have gauged the suitability for wheelchairs from either personal observation or by speaking to the route designers - few natural paths are suitable along the whole of their length.

Most paths become slippery after rain and some which follow bridleways can be impossible to negotiate in wet weather unless you have the correct footwear. The general rule is to take stout boots or shoes unless the weather is very dry.

Regarding general terrain, there is nothing to fear from any of Worcestershire's gentle gradients. Even the rocky Malverns are only 1394 feet at their highest point and can be tackled easily by young children.

Site description: Over fifty sites are described in detail, a personal selection of the most accessible areas of the county. They include woods, commons, Country Parks, hills and valleys and all have one thing in common - they are eminently explorable. Many are reserves of the WNCT or owned by the County Council, in which case, you can wander freely. However there are a number of privately owned sites included for their beauty or exceptional interest on which you must keep to public rights of way. My criterion for including these has been that they must have at least two public footpaths crossing them so that you can explore them in depth. For this reason, some large woods are excluded because they only border rights of way. The status of private sites is, where known, indicated at each account heading. If landowners permit access off rights of way, such as on Wychbury Hill, I have noted this in the site description. Public rights of way are legally for the purpose of "passing and re-passing", and do not include permission to picnic. If this sounds a little offputting, it must be said that many landowners are obliging and will, if asked, allow you to stop on their land. Even though the summit of Bredon Hill is private property, people are allowed to wander where they will.

The individual site descriptions can only hint at what you will find and are aimed at providing a general impression of the area. Local history, geology and natural history are included, the last in more detail since you are likely to see more evidence of it. Several places are nature reserves containing rare or declining wildlife, so please respect it by taking care not to damage the environment.

With so many sites from which to choose, it is inevitable that some have been excluded. I have left out most commons under ten acres in extent, since the exploration potential of these is limited. Similarly rivers and canals are excluded unless they border a more accessible site: a list of river and canal access points is included in the appendix. If your favourite areas are missing I plead lack of space, but this does allow you the satisfaction of discovering new sites for yourself - good hunting!

Wildlife by the Way

For many walkers in the countryside, encounters with wildlife are an unexpected bonus. We can all plan routes past this wood or that folly, but animals are a different matter: who can tell if a fox or hare is around the next bend or if a kingfisher will be watching from a riverside willow? Such happenstance sightings are often the most memorable part of any exploration and the purpose of this chapter is to suggest the creatures, not all of them welcome, that you are likely to meet in Worcestershire. Rarer or more elusive wildlife is mentioned in the appropriate site descriptions.

Woodland: It is not only the wood that you can't see for the trees - wildlife is often invisible too and walking through neglected coppice or dark conifer groves can be a dispiriting experience. Fortunately most of the woods described here are ancient broad-leaved woodlands rich in wildlife. The very best are those managed as coppice with wide rides and sunlit clearings where you can see both into the depths of the wood and have views of the sky above.

It is ironic that one of our most conspicuous woodland animals is a naturalised alien. Grey squirrels were introduced to Britain in the mid-1870s as an ornament to large estates, where they soon bred and flourished, colonising most lowland parts of the country. North American in origin , they are too often accused of ousting the native red squirrel which can no longer be found in Worcestershire. In fact the decline of the red is probably linked to disease and habitat changes and the adaptable grey has merely filled the niches its European cousin once occupied. Foresters have little admiration for this adaptability: grey squirrels can wreak havoc in new plantations by stripping bark from young trees. They can now be found in all of the county's woodlands where they scold loudly from the treetops as you pass beneath.

Other woodland mammals are considerably more elusive. The musky reek of a fox can often be smelt along a footpath, but you are less likely to glimpse its maker. Fallow deer are common in the Wyre Forest and very occasionally seen in woods at Clent and Trimpley. You are more likely to catch sight of a muntjac, a Labrador-sized deer from India which spread from Woburn where it was introduced around 1900. Now many woods in the county harbour this diminutive deer best seen at dusk when the males bark loudly. Their presence is easily detected by the footprints or "slots" along muddy paths or by forest pools. Badgers are our best-known woodland mammal, but very rarely seen, even by naturalists. Should you find a sett, keep its location to yourself or inform the Worcestershire Badger

Group, contactable through the WNCT.

Birds in woodland are a different matter. In spring, resident numbers are swelled by an influx of migrants urgently singing to establish territory. However, the large numbers are not always easy to find and certain species are far more prominent than others. In all woods with mature trees you are almost certain to find great spotted woodpeckers. Black and white with splashes of crimson, the males announce their presence with bursts of springtime drumming and sharp "kik" calls. Summer leaves render them invisible, but their penchant for dead trees as nest-sites and the querulous calls of the nestlings usually betray them to observers. Green woodpeckers are also common throughout Worcestershire, especially in open woods on light, acid soils where their prey, ants, can be found. These birds are often flushed from anthills and bound off showing red heads and yellow rumps; many alleged parrot records are explained by green woodpeckers. No parrot was ever this noisy! Not for nothing is it named the yaffle and you can hear the maniacal calls in winter and spring .

Winter reveals many birds in the bare branches, in particular roving parties of tits. Blue, great and long-tailed tits are common in all deciduous woods. Coal tits, immaculately grey, black and white, are conifer specialists where they consort with goldcrests and siskins. Hangers-on in the tit flocks include treecreepers, brown mouse-like birds which inch in spirals around tree-trunks, and nuthatches , the only British birds which can move up and down a tree with equal agility.

These birds don't band together for sociability. Their conspicuousness attracts predators, but their numbers decrease the chances of being caught since a hawk may be confused when confronted by so many fast-moving choices. Sparrowhawks are more common in Worcestershire now than for many decades. As recently as the mid-1970s, they were a notable sight and the county population had dipped to less than ten pairs. The causes of this huge decline were the organochlorine pesticides containing dieldrin and DDT which were absorbed into the hawks' systems from their songbird prey who in turn had eaten contaminated grain. Such pesticides accumulate in the body fats of birds of prey, causing them to lay thin-shelled eggs which break before hatching. Now that these pesticides have been banned, sparrowhawks are increasing rapidly in wooded areas and are a familiar sight as they soar over clearings. The sexes show marked differences- males are slate-grey with orange-barred underparts and are only slightly larger than a mistle thrush. Females are liver-brown and dove-sized. Both sexes have a distinctive flap-glide flight pattern making them easy to distinguish at great distances.

Butterflies are the most obvious woodland insects, though many species are in decline in the county. Malvern, Wyre Forest and a few special woods harbour exotic orange fritillaries such as the silver-washed and the pearl-

11

bordered. A similar tawny butterfly is the comma, which, with its relatives, the small tortoiseshell and the peacock, may be seen in all Worcestershire woods and open spaces too.

An unwelcome insect for any walker is the cleg, a dull grey-brown fly which lurks in damp woods. It senses your presence well before you are aware of it and delivers a painful bite- make sure you take insect repellent with you when walking through woods in summer.

Open Country: As with woodland, the most noticeable mammal of open country is an introduction. Rabbits were brought to Britain during the 12th century from the western Mediterranean to be bred as a source of meat and fur. The rest, as they say, is history. Rabbit plagues became so serious a threat to agriculture that drastic measures have been employed to control their numbers. In the 1950s the myxoma virus was introduced from Uruguay and took deadly hold. Over 95% of British rabbits perished within five years. The surviving populations developed immunity and have now built up to high levels once more. You will occasionally meet infected animals in the last stages of myxomatosis when they are blind and slow-moving and oblivious of your approach. A re-introduction of a more potent strain of the virus will be bad news for the buzzard, now more common in Worcestershire than for forty years.

Few other mammals are likely to be seen, but foxes, stoats and weasels are all widespread and give occasional glimpses. Brown hares are decidedly scarce and have declined in response to agricultural practices which remove weeds from arable land. On Bredon Hill they are still frequent and there are signs of a very recent increase in parts of the county. In bare March fields you may be lucky enough to see hares "boxing", usually two females disputing a mate.

If there was an "index of conspicuousness" for British birds, the magpie would feature high on the list. Much maligned, this piebald crow has increased dramatically during this century and in doing so has garnered a bad reputation for killing game and songbirds. Despite a recent BTO report exonerating the bird from its suspected crimes, persecution continues. Another very obvious countryside bird is the woodpigeon, large and grey with white bands on each wing. Check the flocks on autumn stubble carefully and you may find stock doves, smaller and without the white bars. Intermingled with these pigeons are the inevitable rooks, crows and jackdaws and a host of smaller birds. Finches and buntings provide opportunities for bumping up your score in winter when they range over open land. Chaffinches, greenfinches and linnets are all well-distributed, though weed seed eaters have declined because of herbicide use and stubble-burning. 1992 was the last year for legal stubble-burning and its banning coupled with the increase in "set-aside" may favour farmland birds.

Game birds are well-established in Worcestershire, a great shooting county. Red-legged partridges and pheasants are released in large numbers to supplement breeding birds and can be seen wherever the crop has been cut and fields ploughed. Grey partridges usually stand out as brown hummocks in winter fields and in spring can be heard creaking from weedy sites.

In summer, ears are as good as eyes in detecting birds. Skylarks sing their "silver chain of song with many breaks" over pasture and arable across the county and yellowhammers wheeze from hedgerows everywhere. A scarce but conspicuous bird of open country, especially barley-growing areas is the corn bunting, drab and sparrow-like. Its song is a chaffy crackle, accelerating like a free-wheeling bicycle and is delivered from a tall vantage point, making location of the buntings an easy affair.

Upland walkers will soon encounter meadow pipits, also drab and streaky which rise and fall monotonously in their spring song-flights. Kestrels, slim and rakish, hunt over high and low ground when their hovering habit will instantly identify them

A wide variety of butterflies and moths frequent open land. The commonest are the meadow brown, the gatekeeper and the ubiquitous small, large and green-veined white butterflies. Day-flying moths include a red-and-black duo, the burnet moths and the cinnabar. Both are brightly coloured, flaunting their poisonous nature: the last is particularly welcomed by farmers as its larva eats ragwort.

Along the Severn and Avon valleys, you will hear the tinny chirpings of dark bush-crickets, audible from a passing car, and in mild years persisting into November.

Rivers and Streams: Riverside walking can yield a surprising flush of wildlife, though a cautious approach is necessary to see most of it. Although otters have begun a tentative return to Worcestershire, it falls to yet another alien to be the most obvious riparian mammal. Since the 1930s, mink have spread along most of our waterways having escaped from commercial fur-farms. With few competitors they are a serious threat to wildfowl and are still hunted by hounds in the west of the county.

After mild winters, many river birds increase and may easily be seen. The recent run of snowless winters has favoured kingfishers and grey herons which starve if their feeding pools ice over. Kingfishers are now common along most unpolluted rivers and streams, but are hard to spot unless you know the call, a sharp whistling "chik-ee". Once you hear this, wait and the bird will soon fly past, arrow-straight and just above the surface. Other likely river birds are moorhens, coots and the delicate grey wagtail which breeds along western streams.

The most beautiful waterside insects are dragonflies, now recorded by the newly-formed Worcestershire Dragonfly Group. Look out for the delicate blue damselflies, the bronze-winged brown hawker and the green southern hawker as well as the red-bodied common darter.

Northern Hills

The hills of north Worcestershire create a natural boundary between the largely rural county to the south and the vast west Midlands conurbation to the north. Their closeness to the city makes them familiar and much-loved stamping-grounds for urban dwellers who visit them to enjoy the wide-ranging views across town and country. Access is generally excellent thanks to the Country Parks of Kingsford, Clent, Waseley and Lickey which are linked by the North Worcestershire Path.

Kingsford Country Park

The Staffordshire and Worcestershire Canal

Wychbury Hill

Clent Hills Country Park
Adams Hill
Walton Hill

Uffmoor Wood

Waseley Hills Country Park

Lickey Hills Country Park
Bilberry Hill
Beacon Hill

Kingsford Country Park

OSL Map 138
GR SO 836/821
Kingsford Car Park

OSP SO 88/98
GR SO 824/822
Blakeshall Lane Car Park

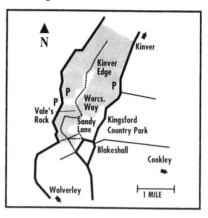

HWCS On minor roads north of Wolverley Village. 200 acres of birch woods, pine and larch plantations and heathland. Excellent walking and views across Worcestershire/Shropshire and Staffordshire borders. Paths good. Short and steep ascent from Kingsford Lane.

What better place to begin an exploration of Worcestershire than on its north-western frontier at Kingsford. This Country Park is managed by HWCS as a recreation area and a working forest- over 160 acres are dedicated to conifer plantation. If this were its only attraction, Kingsford would be dull indeed, but the place has a few surprises up its sleeve.

Although the Black Country can clearly be seen through the trees, Kingsford is comparatively isolated in a network of narrow roads that weave in and out of Staffordshire and Shropshire. Most visitors stumble upon it by accident from the hugely popular Kinver Edge which adjoins the

Country Park. From the B4189 at Wolverley the Park is signposted; alternatively you can approach it from the north at Kinver and take the minor road west of the Edge. There are car-parks in Blakeshall Lane, north of Wolverley and Kingsford Lane. Your choice of parking place may depend on how strenuous you wish the walk to be - the Kingsford Lane approach requires a short, but very steep climb to the Edge. This description takes the gentler route from Blakeshall Lane where you begin amid the sheltering groves of larch trees.

As you will soon see, the soil is very sandy here and is derived from the Triassic deserts which once covered the area. Few plants can grow in these acid conditions, but conifers such as larch, Norway spruce and Scots pine are completely at home. The cool stands of conifers are a welcome change from the tightly-packed plantations usually met with, and have an understorey of ferns, holly and elder bushes. In spring they are alive with singing chaffinches, goldcrests (our smallest bird) and blackcaps. Occasionally jays will betray the roost of a tawny owl, hunched against the trunk to avoid being seen.

The paths, velvet with pine-needles underfoot, soon reach the sandstone ridge of Kinver Edge, an excellent viewpoint across ancient countryside. Small fields and copses stretch far into Shropshire beyond Castle Hill where King John once had a hunting-lodge, hence the name Kingsford. This is an important junction for long-distance walkers since it marks the beginnings of three Regional Routes; the 92 mile Staffordshire Way leading north to Mow Cop, the 39 mile Worcestershire Way heading southwards to Malvern and the North Worcestershire which ends its journey near Solihull, 27 miles to the east.

If you walk along the Edge you enter Staffordshire, where the National Trust have cut back invading birch and pine trees to allow the heather to flourish. Open heath is a delicate habitat, requiring careful management and would soon disappear if left to itself, swamped by surrounding trees. By conserving the heath the Trust wardens are hoping to tempt back a declining bird, the nightjar, whose eldritch reeling was once such a feature of this heathland. It is likely that other,

unknown factors are keeping the birds away, but there is still a possibility that one summer night you may hear them churring again.

The paths which descend from the ridge are steep and pebbly, but go down you must if you wish to see Worcestershire's best rock-house. Vale's Rock lies on the county boundary and is an enormous outcrop of weathered red sandstone. Examine it more closely and you will see the hollowed-out rooms in which generations of troglodytes have lived since the 17th century. The last occupant of Vale's Rock, a besom maker, left as recently as 1961 and had piped water and gas connected to what must have been a snug and very picturesque dwelling. Now the gaunt ruin has suffered from vandalism - the friable stone has been worn away and the roof is supported by metal props. Children love to explore the rock-houses, but should be watched carefully - the sandstone is slippery at all times and the drops are sheer - please take great care.

Below the rock-houses is an expanse of birch-trees, slim and graceful. Few of them are old- like rock stars, birches die young. They all seem to be of a similar age even though they are mixed with older oaks - why is this?. Look more closely and you will notice that many, even young trees, are dead. They have been attacked by the birch polypore or razor-strop fungus, a deadly bracket fatal to birches of all ages. When the trees are rotten, they make perfect nest-sites for hole-nesters such as woodpeckers, marsh tits and nuthatches, all common birds here. A speciality is the redstart, a summer migrant from Africa with an orange tail and black mask. The males arrive in late April and sing from the treetops to attract mates. Following them are wood warblers, slim green-and-yellow birds which utter a shivering trill from among the birch twigs.

To the south of the birchwoods is a small patch of heathland, recently cleared by HWCS rangers. In sunny places, common lizards bask and green tiger beetles hunt for insects along the paths.

Step along the bridleway into the pines and the world changes, Even in mid-summer, this is a cool place, dark and featureless, but strangely atmospheric. Sandy outcrops lie forgotten in the gloom. Strange fungi sprout from a carpet of slowly-decaying nee-dles. The only bird sounds are the needling pinpricks of coal tits invisible among the cloaking branches. It's a silent sunless world, fascinating yet sinister, a modern Mirkwood. When a splash of colour does appear it is more than welcome, even if happens to be highly poisonous. Fly agaric toadstools grow in the sandy shade, incongruous splashes of red and orange flecked with the creamy fragments of the cap-sheath. They rarely kill, but are strongly hallucinogenic and addictive; Lapps lure their reindeer down from the hills by leaving a trail of dried agarics for them.

The paths through the conifers lead either uphill to the ridgetop or along the route of the Worcestershire way to Sandy Lane. If you follow this you will soon emerge on Blakeshall lane about half a mile from the car-park and your starting-point.

Staffordshire & Worcestershire Canal

OSL Map 139
GR Caunsall Bridge 856/809

OSP SO 88/98

Approach from A449 north of Cookley.

Canal towpath walking, muddy in places, but flat throughout. Marsh and riverside, but suitable for prams and pushchairs.

Public transport: Bus from Kidderminster to Caunsall.

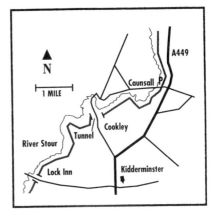

When the Parliamentary Act permitting the "Staffs. and Worcester" to be built was passed in 1766, the last intention was to create a habitat for wildlife. And when the celebrated engineer and surveyor, James Brindley planned the course of the waterway between Haywood Junction and Stourport, he had in mind the transport of Midland coal and iron, not tourists. Now, the canal is a popular walking, cruising and fishing venue and its first four Worcestershire miles are among the most beautiful in the county.

With its restricted towpaths - and these are as narrow as any - the Staffs. and Worcester is hardly an open space, but the route described here includes at least one useful picnic spot where you and your family can wander more freely. Care is needed on the towpath if you have small children and, needless to say, stout footwear is essential after rain and in winter.

The walk begins at Caunsall Bridge immediately west of the A449. Limited car-parking is available beyond the steeply-arched bridge, though you may have to jostle for space in the coarse fishing season between mid-June and mid-March.

Head south and you find yourself enclosed by willow groves and pasture bordering the River Stour. Once these were lush and marshy and flooded in winter so that in places they were impassable. Now, a mere thirty years on, things have changed. The Stour has been drained, the water table lowered and the meadows grazed heavily. Only a handful of yellow iris remain, stolid survivors in a sea of grass.

The first bridge at Clay House is a scheduled ancient monument, now cowering under the shadow of Westley Court, a huge and incongruous red-brick home for retired people. Sites for static caravans crowd the water's edge until you reach the second bridge and the spectacular Austcliffe Rock.

Twenty-five feet of Bunter sandstone looms over the canal at an angle which threatens to crash into the water at any minute- not for nothing is it known locally as Hanging Rock. In 1990, British Waterways Board removed a large portion to prevent a likely accident. This is an excellent spot in which to observe the layered pebble beds, washed here over 200 million years ago. So narrow is the canal at this point that an overflow has been constructed to channel excess rainwater into the Stour. Lively though the river sounds, it is not a pleasant prospect. Cloudy with pollution from its Black Country headwaters its malodorous meanders are cut between steep banks.

Austcliffe Rock

Amazingly these are home for kingfishers and grey wagtails which nest here but wisely feed along the canal.

Beyond Hanging Rock, you enter the outskirts of Cookley. Wildlife is surprisingly rich; noctule and pipistrelle bats hawk for insects on summer evenings and little owls yelp from old osier beds. At the entrance to Cookley Tunnel are a number of wych elms where, if you are lucky you may see a white-letter hairstreak butterfly. This is a binoculars-only insect, tiny and brown and high-flying. Its cousin, the purple hairstreak, can also be seen here around oak trees in July and August.

Brindley decided to route his tunnel through the ridge of sandstone on which Cookley stands and its 65 yards make it the longest on the canal and the oldest in Worcestershire. At its other end is the former steel stampings factory whose origins, in the form of an ironworks stretch back to 1650; once the Stour was diverted through their grounds to power the machinery.

Behind the factory is Lock Meadow to which Black Country families came on camping holidays until as recently as the 1960s. Pitching their tents would cause problems nowadays; the site has been bulldozed, ostensibly to create a car-park for employees, but as yet fly-ash and weeds are all you can see.

At Debdale Lock there is an in-habited lock-cottage and a footbridge leading to Cookley playing fields. Caves in the red sandstone may have been carved to shelter canal-diggers from the elements. If you long for open space away from the confines of the towpath, cross the footbridge and relax in the peaceful surroundings of the playing fields. It's the perfect place for a picnic or, in summer, to enjoy a village cricket match - Cookley takes its cricket seriously. Views from the acid grassland take in Wolverley, Kidderminster and the heathland ridge of Kinver Edge. Go in May and the two venerable oaks are encircled by sweeps of white meadow saxifrage, a scarce plant of old pasture.

Back on the canal, the path heads south, shadowing the river. Sandy outcrops and neglected osier beds lend a wild feel to this section, accentuated by the craggy oaks which are probably three hundred years old. A gap in the alders and willows marks the route of the Elan Valley pipeline which once carried millions of gallons daily over the iron bridge to serve the needs of Birmingham and neighbouring towns.

Trees take over for the next half-mile, arguably the most beautiful stretch of the waterway. Beech, sycamore and oaks are mirrored in the still water. In autumn fogs, when pleasure crafts have moored for the season, this is a tranquil spot, full of damp humours emanating from the alder groves. Alders spread rapidly in this sodden acid earth, their seeds dispersed by winter spates. Any remaining on the twigs are prised loose by the sharp beaks of siskins and redpolls which swarm in the treetops. Few marsh plants grow in alder shade because they have been crowded out by Himalayan balsam. The gardeners who introduced this showy, pink annual to Britain in 1839 unwittingly unleashed a vegetable monster into the countryside. Its succulent and fast-growing stems reach a height of up to ten feet in a couple of months and are topped by a cluster of exploding seed capsules. The WNCT organises regular balsam-bashing parties to protect their reserves, but the battle is a tough one as witness the regiments of fleshy stems lining most county river banks.

Himalayan Balsam

Between the aqueduct and Wolverley lock is the old forge dating from the 17th century. Once a corn mill a century previously, it flourished under the influence of the canal and had its own wharf. Earlier this century, the mill wheel drove a generator supplying electricity to a nearby house. The nine workman's cottages no longer survive but the forge buildings have been sensitively converted into private houses.

A short walk takes you to the Lock Inn and welcome refreshment. If you want a longer stroll, there are two choices. Under the main road, the canal continues for a mile to the outskirts of Kidderminster. The grazing marshes at Stourvale are almost the last remnants of the pre-drainage landscape and shelter southern marsh orchids in dwindling numbers. Beyond is the industrial architecture of Kidderminster town.

Alternatively, take a right turn for a hundred yards or so, then right again into the curious village of Wolverley. With its tiny cottages gouged from the sandstone and bizarre Italianate houses, this is a fascinating place to visit. To regain the canal you may either retrace your steps or walk through the deep sandy cutting past the Live and let Live hotel. Follow the first no-through road on your right and take the public footpath to the right next to the last dwelling. This crosses a field, enters Gloucester Coppice and emerges at Wolverley forge. The canal towpath lies to the right along a narrow path.

Wychbury Hill

OSL Map 139 GR 918/818

OSP SO 88/98

Off A456 1 mile north of Hagley.

Approach from Pedmore Hall Lane along public footpath. Limited parking at GR 922/823.

Private. Wooded hill fort surrounded by open grassland and pasture. Noted for its follies erected by George. First Lord Lyttelton. Paths good, muddy in wet weather - some shallow climbing from Pedmore.

Public transport: Buses from Birmingham and Halesowen to Kidderminster pass the hill.

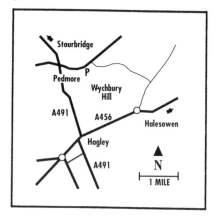

First the good news- Wychbury Hill is a beautiful, partly wooded eminence presiding over Hagley. Its mature trees shelter an Iron Age hill fort and a splendid 18th Century folly. Wide-ranging views take in the Wrekin, the Malverns and the Black Country. Despite the busy A456, it is a remarkably tranquil place, well-loved by local walkers.

Now the bad news. Wychbury lies directly in the path of a proposed Hagley by-pass which will drive a six-lane highway through the heart of the hill, ruining the atmosphere for walkers and local inhabitants. The road has been planned in response to complaints from frontages along the A456 in Hagley that traffic is too heavy. This has certainly increased beyond all measure, but it is sad that residents who presumably value Hagley for its semi-rural location are prepared to so easily compromise the countryside beyond their back gates. Not all residents feel like this - a vigorous action group has been formed to oppose the road. We can only hope that they are successful in preventing what amounts to irredeemable vandalism by the Department of Transport.

For such an accessible place, parking is very limited. Footpaths run from the traffic island on the A456 and from the top of Monument Lane, but the easiest way to avoid congestion is to walk uphill along the public footpath from Pedmore Hall Lane, where you can park on a residential road. This path brings you to the crown of the hill and straight ahead is Wychbury's famous landmark. The Hagley "Monument" is a sandstone obelisk erected at the instruction of George, 1st Lord Lyttelton in the mid-18th Century. Stand beneath the monument and you have splendid views of Hagley Hall, the family seat which he built between 1756 and 1760. A solid Palladian block of symmetrical sandstone, the house is still the family home of the Lytteltons and stands in naturalistic grounds landscaped by Sanderson Miller.

Several follies remain including a sham castle high on the Clent Hills opposite and below you on Wychbury itself, the Temple of Theseus, the first Greek revivalist building in Britain. Although there are no footpaths to either the temple or the obelisk, the Lyttelton estate allows access to considerate visitors. Sadly, vandals have damaged both edifices in recent years and there have been threats of closure to walkers.

One intriguing piece of graffiti on the crumbling obelisk reads "Who put Bella in the wych elm?" and refers to the discovery in the 1930's of a woman's head in a hollow tree nearby. Her body turned up in another tree, but her murderer and identity remain unknown to this day. She was christened Bella by the police and the tree in which she was found has provided us with the most botanically precise graffiti in the county!

One last monumental fact; because the obelisk is a folly it is often cruelly likened by non-residents to the people of Hagley - stuck up for no reason and not quite straight.

Back under the screening sycamores are the dramatic earthworks of Wychbury Ring, bisected by the West Midlands county boundary. Defended by a double bank and ditches, this Iron Age hill fort was once a busy community of the Dobunni tribe who controlled the surrounding countryside. No recent excavations have been undertaken but fragments of bronze horse harnesses dated to the early Iron Age were unearthed in 1884. Some local historians claim that the hill was the burial place of King Arthur, a theory which has received plenty of airing following the by-pass threat. Walk around the ramparts beneath the venerable yews and you'll find it a seductive argument. No matter that, yews excepted, the native trees have been largely felled or that laurel and rhododendrons have been planted as game cover. Wychbury has a brooding resonance which we should enjoy while we are able.

Clent Hills Country Park

OSL Map 139

OSP SO 88/98

On minor roads off A456. Signposted from A456 at Hayley Green. Car parks at Nimmings Plantation off Hagley Wood Lane (Ref. SO938807); Walton Hill (Ref.943803) and Adam's Hill (Ref. SO 926798).

Public toilets at Nimmings Plantation and Adam's Hill.

Nearly 500 acres of grassland and woodland including a working farm. Much is common land owned by National Trust and Hereford & Worcester County Council and managed by the Council's Countryside Service.

Public transport: Regular bus service to Hayley Green and Hagley along A456.

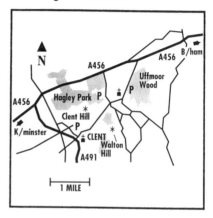

Britain's second busiest Country Park needs little introduction to the residents of the West Midlands who have been visiting these beautiful hills for generations. Now owned by the National Trust and managed by HWCC's Countryside Service, they comprise nearly 500 acres of invaluable common land over which you may wander freely. Small wonder then, that they are so popular; 900,000 visitors come each year to enjoy the prospects and if you go on a summer bank holiday, you could be forgiven for thinking that they are all there at once!

However, don't let crowds and the statutory "Country Park" signs put you off - Clent has enough woods and hollows to absorb any amount of visitors, and in the week it is possible to explore the bracken-clad hillsides without meeting another person.

There are two hills, Walton and Clent, the latter also called Adams' Hill. They are divided by a deep and picturesque valley known as Clatterbach or St. Kenelm's Pass. Both are capped with a coarse sandstone in a marly matrix which takes its name from the hills. Clent breccia was deposited here around 270 million years ago and gives footpaths across the park their characteristic redness. The small stream draining Clatterbach must once have been more powerful since it supplied energy for a string of nail-making workshops.

Here each hill is treated as a distinct location, but of course many people walk the entire circuit (about three miles) and a hardy few run the distance. Before you don your running-shoes though, it's well worth taking a stroll around Clent village. Rare amongst Worcestershire place-names, Clent retains to this day its original Domesday Book spelling. Its centre is surprisingly unspoilt, dwarfed by the hills and bounded by the A456 motorway feeder road. St. Leonard's church is the focal point; if you look carefully you may just spot the grooves in its sandstone tower created when oak branches were hauled to the top each May 29th. This is Oak-apple Day, a celebration of King Charles the Second's restoration to the throne: his deliverance was in part due to the sheltering canopy of an oak, though its exact location is hotly disputed.

At the opposite end of the parish, beyond the top of Clatterbach, is St. Kenelm's church, all that remains of the lost settlement of Kenelmstowe. To the right of the church is an inconspicuous damp hollow, the source not only of a spring, but of the lost settlement also and one of the county's strangest tales. It has enough violence, aristocracy and intrigue to merit a prime-time series on modern television and it all happened at this spot.

In 819 A.D. King Kenulf of Mercia died leaving a seven year old heir, Kenelm. The boy's elder sister Quendryda conspired with his tutor Ascobert to murder her brother and so gain control of the kingdom. During a hunting expedition, the boy was decapitated by a swordstroke and buried by the murderer in a shallow grave. Quendryda succeeded to the kingdom and for a while all was forgotten. Her explanations about Kenelm's death failed to satisfy some of her subjects however, and suspicions grew when divine forces intervened. A white cow began to keep vigil over a thorn-bush, returning to the same place each day, after giving twice its normal quota of milk; thereafter the spot was called Cowbach. Next a white dove appeared before the Pope bearing a scroll on which was written;

'In Clent, in Cowbach, lyeth
under a thorn
His head off-shorn, Kenelm,
King born'

Such signs could hardly be ignored and, guided by the cow, messengers disinterred the boy's body. It was conveyed in a coffin to Winchcombe in Gloucestershire, and a spring gushed forth in the place where the body had been. When Quendryda saw the coffin she tried to show her contempt for the burial service by reciting the 108th psalm backwards, upon which her eyes started from their sockets and she fell down dead. Pilgrims began to visit the spring and St.Kenelm's church was built to accommodate their prayers.

Having sampled the surrounding attractions - to the hills!

Adams' Hill

There are two main access points for Adams' Hill. At the southern end, near Clent village is a turning next to the Fountain Inn. This no-through road leads to a small car-park, a hotel (the Hill Tavern) and an amusement arcade. Paths wind slowly and steeply to the summit, but this route is not really recommended, being unattractive and badly eroded. It is well-frequented by sledgers in the increasingly rare snow-showers, but its slopes have been dotted with caged trees, presumably to allow the turf to recover.

By contrast, the northern car-park at Nimmings Plantation is pleasant and well-landscaped. It is sign-posted from the A456 at Hayley Green and reached by a tortuously steep lane. Maps and information boards are provided by the Countryside Service who have also installed an easy-access trail which allows wheelchairs to reach the toposcope. This gravelled trail remains firm in the wettest weather and offers as good a route as any to the summit. The first section is through beech woodland.

Beeches crown the hill like the crest on a centurion's helmet, and these, planted as a landscape feature, are each carved with a direc-tory of visitors' names. In autumn the thick beechmast crunches underfoot attracting bramblings, Scandinavian finches with a penchant for the seeds. Larch plantations soon take over, light and airy and fresh emerald in spring. Larch is an important commercial timber at Clent, a softwood used for pulping and chipping as well as the familiar garden fencing.

As you emerge from the trees superb views appear to the south over a sea of bracken and rose bay willowherb. Few plants will grow on the impoverished breccia soil, so the ardent botanist may well be disappointed. No disappointments with the panorama from the toposcope though - the Clee Hills and the Wrekin lie to the west, the Malverns and Bredon to the south-east. On a clear day you can even make out the truncated whaleback of the Black Mountains on the Welsh border. Nearer at hand are Wychbury obelisk and the parkland of Hagley Hall. The sham castle close at hand is a folly, placed there at the bequest of George, first lord Lyttelton who built the hall between 1756 and 1760. Used as a summer-house by the family until recently, it was constructed from the stones of the derelict St. Mary's Abbey at Lapal near Halesowen. There is no public access to Hagley Park, though villagers were once allowed to stroll in the landscaped grounds that Alexander Pope admired.

Wheelchair access is difficult beyond the toposcope where the path becomes stony and uneven. Turn sharp left and ahead are the Four Stones, at the highest point of the hill, almost 1000 feet above sea-level. It is tempting to think that these standing stones are prehistoric monoliths, a sort of mini-henge erected by Druidical zealots. Not so; they were placed here as a focal point by Sanderson Miller who landscaped the hill as an extension of Hagley Park in the mid-18th century.

Nevertheless the stones have been the site of a number of curious rituals, best left unmentioned, as well as being roped off to form a boxing ring!

Paths abound, radiating from the summit so you are spoilt for choice. Many walkers pass straight through on the North Worcestershire Path which crosses the hill en route to Kinver Edge. Most people, however come to revel in the glorious views across the surrounding countryside or to picnic on the grassy slopes. To the south-east is a broad path leading to a newly-created tree collection or arboretum which the Countryside Service will be augmenting in future.

Walton Hill

At 1035 feet, Walton Hill is Worcestershire's second highest point, beaten only by the Malverns. It is less often visited than Adam's Hill and has a wilder feel. To reach it, simply turn right at the top of St. Kenelm's Pass next to High Harcourt Farm. This, incidentally. is a working farm owned by the National Trust and is open to the public on certain days of the year when free guided tours are available. Sheep-worrying is an all too frequent problem, so please remember to keep your dog on a lead.

At Walton Hill car-park you will find the customary maps and signboards erected by the Countryside Service in addition to a

programme of guided walks and events. This hill can also boast its own easy access trail, though you may wish to prove yourself and struggle up one of the lesser routes to the top. Once there look north and the West Midlands conurbation is revealed, spread like an apron before you. Landmarks to pinpoint include Turner's Hill at Oldbury, the MEB headquarters atop Mucklow Hill and Birmingham University's red-brick clock-tower. From here the route to the quaintly-named Moab's Wash Pot, at the summit is broad and flattish. It illustrates perfectly one of Clent's intractable problems - erosion. All those people, whether on foot , horseback or mountain bike, have taken their toll over the years. Grass grows thinly on this poor red soil and cannot recover from the ceaseless tread of generations of visitors. For this reason,horses and mountain bikes are restricted to bridleways marked by a blue arrow and horseshoe sign; you can help by keeping to the paths and avoiding the grassy edges.

Wildlife on Walton is varied. Bird-watchers regularly visit the tops to watch migration in progress and in blustery weather, thrushes and other travellers are temporarily grounded. Ring ouzels turn up annually in spring or autumn, clacking noisily from the rowans. Kestrels hang in the air currents, crucified on the breeze and green woodpeckers probe the springy turf for ants and grubs.

Western gorse is making a comeback, recovering from the disastrous fires which broke out in the long hot summer of 1976. Its spiny branches are home to long-tailed tits, linnets and yellowhammers, all-year round birds which you can find with a little patience.

If you follow the summit path south you will eventually reach a fork, the right-hand prong of which descends steeply to Clent village. Take the alternative route and you reach the hamlet of Walton Pool.

Walton Hill is at its wildest in midwinter, when the kite-fliers and model aeroplane enthusiasts are tucked up indoors. When snow has fallen & the surrounding fields are silvered with frost, it is remote and astonishingly beautiful.

Uffmoor Wood

OSL Map 139
GR 948/811 (Car Park)

OSP SO 88/98

Off A456 at Hayley Green, along Uffmoor Wood Lane. From Clent, south to St Kenelm's Church and left down hill.

Woodland Trust. Ancient semi-natural woodland rich in wildlife. Few views, but fascinating network of paths and rides. Ideal for picnics and exploration. Flat, but muddy in hollows.

Wheelchair access along main ride from car-park.

Public Transport: Buses from Birmingham to Kidderminster. Alight at Hayley Green.

We all have our own ideas of what an ancient wood should look like - massive forest giants towering above impenetrable tangles of underbrush where the sun's rays never reach. Such woods were always populated in fairytales by wolves and other dangerous animals, so it is hardly surprising that we tend to give them a wide berth.

If this is your interpretation, then Uffmoor Wood will, at first glance, be a disappointment. Instead of cathedrals of oak and beech there are over 200 acres of saplings and scrub, mostly under twenty feet high. There is also a car-park, a feature any self-respecting wildwood should instantly disown while between the trees you can see, only too plainly, the rooftops of Halesowen, and beyond them, Birmingham itself.

Appearances, however, can be deceptive. A walk through Uffmoor Wood at any season will soon reveal that this is a very special place indeed and you are walking on land that has probably been wooded since the last Ice Age, over 10,000 years ago.

Uffmoor's apparent youthfulness is explained by its past management. From mediaeval times up to the early 20th Century, it was grown as coppice - with-standards, but this practice was discontinued when the demand for fencing declined and the coppice deteriorated into a tangle of brushwood. An apt term this, for in 1978 Uffmoor was re-planted by a brush-making company which set about growing saplings suitable for turnery. These extensive plantations of alder, ash, poplar and sycamore remain today.

Sadly, public access was banned

until 1986 when Uffmoor was purchased by the Woodland Trust who built a much-needed car-park in Uffmoor Wood Lane and cleared the overgrown rides.

This car-park is an excellent starting point for exploring the wood. As you proceed along the main ride, grassy tunnels between birch and alder shoot off to right and left. A detour along any of these will take you through a maze of bluebelled rides and inevitably into muddy patches - at any season Uffmoor is a wet place. Streams draining from Clent pour into the wood so that in late winter the whole landscape gurgles around you! Boots are a must. All rides inter-connect, so that there is no danger of getting lost, merely the thrill of only half-knowing where you will end up.

The damp red clay and steep-sided rivulets are favoured by some of Worcestershire's rarest plants. One to search for in early summer is water avens, its hanging red lanterns glowing dully along the wettest rides. Later in the summer, the course of the Elan Valley water main comes alive with swarms of common spotted orchids, in all shades from pure white to deep crimson. Other scarce plants in the wood include herb paris and violet and broad-leaved helleborine orchids. Approaching along Uffmoor Wood Lane in spring, you cannot fail to notice the stubby pink spikes of butterbur whose enormous leaves once served as butter-coolers and which double as umbrellas on wet days.

A late evening visit in spring is essential to observe one of Uffmoor's special birds. As the light fades, woodcocks begin their crepuscular territorial flights. These strange waders are unique in Britain in nesting in woodland and announce their presence by roding, the name given to their circular territorial flight, while uttering shrill squeaks and curious grunts. In most years, they are accompanied at dusk by the reeling of grasshopper warblers, tiny summer migrants which lurk deep within the birch thickets. Garden warblers and blackcaps are also common, though in winter are replaced by spluttering parties of long-tailed tits.

You need to tread very carefully in order to see Uffmoor's largest mammal, the fallow deer. Remnants of a population turned loose from nearby Hagley Park during World War Two still visit the wood and damp areas are pitted with their slot-marks.

Take care to avoid treading on the many slugs - one could be the scarce grey-black slug , an inhabitant of very old woods. It's not easy to miss, being jet-black and up to eight inches long!

Waseley Hills Country Park

OSL 508/97
GR SO 972 783

OSL Map 139.

Off Gannow Green Lane, 1 mile west of Rubery. Signposted from M5 Junction 4 and A491

Car parks at Gannow Green Lane (Ref.972783) where visitor centre, picnic area and toilets and cafe. South car park at Holywell Lane (Ref. 979768)

About 150 acres of hilly pasture and woodland on the south-western fringe of Birmingham. Managed by Hereford & Worcester Countryside Service.

Public transport; Regular bus service to Rubery and Romsley (via B4551)

Tucked snugly into a curve of the M5 Motorway to the west and flanked by Rubery to the east, the Waseley Hills are true urban fringe countryside. Their importance to the residents of Birmingham can be seen on busy weekends when the visitor centre, opened by Hereford & Worcester Countryside Service, is thronged with walkers and craftspeople, for Waseley has a flourishing crafts guild.

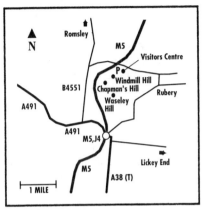

Most visitors come for the spectacular views over Birmingham and the North Worcestershire countryside. In summer the open fields are a Mecca for kite-fliers and in winter their place is taken by skiers or tobogganists. The route of the North Worcestershire Path crosses the hills on its way between Kingsford and Forhill picnic site.

Waseley probably owes its name to the Anglo-Saxon "waer" meaning a sheep, and "ley" a pasture, though nowadays there are more cattle than sheep. Walking while map-reading can be a risky business and there were more than a few participants of a recent nocturnal treasure hunt who returned wishing they had taken torches! Until the 16th Century much of the present park belonged to the estate of nearby Chadwick Manor, itself owned by St, Wul-

33

stan's Hospital, Worcester. Following the Dissolution of the Monasteries, the land was made over to Christchurch by Henry VIII. In 1904 it was bought by the Cadbury family who made over the hillier parts of the land to the National Trust and in 1971 a further parcel of remaining land was purchased by the County Council. Now the hills are cared for by a team of rangers who repair paths, replant hedges and answer your questions!

If you arrive by car the logical place to begin is at the visitor centre in Gannow Green Lane. Ahead of you is the lush slope of Windmill Hill across a sward of rye grass. However, resist the temptation to climb the gentle slope and turn left through the kissing gate, hugging the fence.

On the other side of the old hedge is a damp hollow surrounded by barbed wire. This inauspicious spot is the source of the river Rea, around which Birmingham's first industry burgeoned, humble origins indeed. Waseley is a natural watershed-rain falling to the east drains to the North Sea, to the west into the Bristol Channel.

Boggy flushes are a feature of this hillside, their presence being a result of the local geology. The hills are largely composed of sandy deposits known as Clent Breccia which drains freely. On Waseley the breccia overlies the Keele Beds, bands of poorly-drained gritty clay. In places where the soil types meet, water is forced to the surface where it appears as springs. These wet flushes have a special flora which includes a few plants rare elsewhere in the county. None are particularly spectacular or demonstrative and, like Lewis Carroll's snark, must be pursued with forks and with hope! Tiny and green, blinks has minute white flowers which never really open, hence its name. Ivy-leaved crowfoot is a small white-flowered buttercup which, like blinks, lurks in the wettest places - skulks would be an appropriate name.

To the left as you continue is Birmingham, the foreground dominated by the Longbridge car plant. Ahead are the Lickey Hills, clothed in pines with the grassy slope of Beacon Hill shining out like a bald patch. A small pond on the left of the path was once a claypit, dug as a source of clay for a tile factory in Rubery, now long gone. Local schoolchildren have now adopted the pond as an environmental restoration project-good news for the newts.

Just past the pond turn right up the hillside and right again up the steps by an old ash tree. The turf here is gashed red where cattle erosion has prevented regrowth. You are now in an ancient "green lane", probably an old drover's road across the hills. Hazel and field maples testify to the provenance of this route and there is a fine rowan in the hedge. Hedges on the hills tend to be gappy and poor in species, but this is a reflection of the altitude and grazing pressure rather than youth. In fact, there are some very old hedge-lines on the hills - an excellent example can be seen near the southern car park. Holly bushes are particularly prominent, their presence owing less to superstition than their berries being a source of potential income.

Onwards and upwards. As you reach the crest of the hill, you can begin to appreciate just why Waseley receives so many visitors - the contrasting vistas of town and country are fascinating. Behind is the Birmingham plateau, its uniformity relieved by tower blocks and the twin spires of the post office building and the brick campanile of the university. In front are the wooded spines of Abberley and Woodbury Hills. Taking the path to the summit of Windmill Hill brings you to the circular toposcope, an interpretation of the surrounding countryside. Among the eminences picked out are the Clent Hills and Black Country ridge to the east, the Shropshire Clees, the Long Mynd and Caer Caradoc. A small tuft of trees on a near hill are the Frankley beeches. They lie at the other side of the motorway which never allows you to ignore its proximity.

From this point, it's all downhill to return to the visitor centre and a welcome snack. However, many Waseley walkers come to see the bluebells in Segbourne Coppice which lies at the bottom of one of the valleys on the southern flanks of the country park. Local children know this area as "Gypsy Meadow", though it has little to do with travellers; the copse was a burial place for Gyp, a dog owned by the Cadburys, which died in 1934. The pond, excavated by rangers and schoolchildren, won a Shell "Better Britain" award.

To the North of the Segbourne Coppice pond, through the trees, is a second valley, worth a visit in Summer. Rabbits have reached plague proportions here and the hedgebottoms are a honeycomb of burrows where few plants can grow. They do keep tall vegetation in check though, and are responsible for the clouds of common blue and small copper butterflies abundant in July and August.

The footpaths from these two valleys lead onto the Chadwich Manor estate and to regain the north car park, you need to retrace your steps via Windmill Hill. Alternatively, you can head southwards to the top of Waseley Hill, at 1013 feet, the highest point in the country park.

Lickey Hills

The tramlines stop at Rednal: they are still there though the trams have not run since the 1950s. Buses and cars now bring the residents of Birmingham to the Lickey Hills, out on the A38, past the old British Leyland factory. Worcestershire countryside they may be, but Birmingham has made the Lickeys its own, to the extent of purchasing around 500 acres for public recreation.

Exploring the four hills of the Country Park for the first time, you have the impression of not really leaving the suburbs. Rubery and Rednal march right up to their feet and the oak and beech woods are dotted with the gables of exclusive Victorian residences. You can never quite "get away from it all". Nevertheless Lickey remains an attractive place, definitely worth visiting, though it's

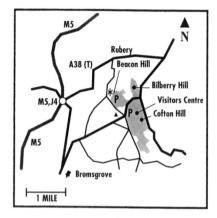

useful to remember that at weekends it can become busy.

There are two broad areas to make for, at Beacon Hill and Bilberry Hill. Here they are dealt with individually, but you can walk a complete circuit comfortably in a morning.

Bilberry Hill

OSL Map 139
GR SO 997/754

OSP SO 87/97

Access to visitor centre from B4096 at Rednal, south of Birmingham.

BCC: Birch woodland, conifer plantations and hillside. Beech and oak woods at Lickey Warren. Good walking with steps along steeper slopes. Visitor centre with car park for disabled, refreshments and toilets.

Public transport: Bus from Birmingham and Bromsgrove to Rednal.

Unless you know the hills intimately, the best place in which to start your exploration is the visitor centre at Bilberry Hill. This is located in Warren Lane and is well signposted from the B4096 Rednal to Bromsgrove road. Here there is ample parking, refreshments and an information desk manned by the Council's rangers. Nearby is an arboretum and, very useful in indifferent weather, a play area for children. Inside the centre, you can obtain self-guided trails and facts and figures about the hills. The Ranger service operates a programme of events and walks for all ages and interests, check the notice-boards for details.

The big advantage of beginning here is soon realised when you leave the car-park and climb a few paces; you are nearly at the top already! Bilberry Hill is 900 feet above sea-level with commanding views to the east and north. It is composed of hard quartzite rock, thought until recently to be Cambrian, but now believed to be of Ordovician origin. Tough and durable, it was deposited between 515 and 445 million years ago and colours the pathways greyish-white. Heather and bilberries thrive on the Quartzite and there are places on Bilberry Hill which resemble the best Scottish hillsides. Dense groves of Scots pines add to this impression, overlaying the ground with a carpet of noise-killing needles. On winter afternoons, the sunlight catches ranks of pine trunks, suffusing them with a russet glow.

Head north from the centre and viewpoint and you reach a steep drop. Below is the Old Birmingham road, to which leads a vertiginous flight of downward-facing steps. Walking up these is a breathtaking procedure since they lean towards you: think twice about approaching the hills from this angle! Beyond the road is the pine-covered hummock of Rednal Hill from which you can see southern Birmingham and the flat roofs of the Austin Rover works.

The view from Bilberry Hill to the west takes in Beacon Hill and the golf course below. Its fairways are corrugated like green card, and this has furnished local historians with enough evidence to uncover a crime several centuries old. Once, the Lickeys were part of the Royal Forest of Feckenham. Commoners holding land within its purlieu were forbidden to cultivate their holding without the permission of the lord of the manor. One commoner was apparently successful in ploughing an area of woodland hidden deep within the trees, and his illegal assarting, that is the creation of farmland from existing heath or wood, is shown to this day as "ridge and furrow". Be sure your sins will find you out!

The original wildwood has long since disappeared, banished in favour of commercial conifer and hard wood plantations. Most of the pines were planted by the Earl of Plymouth, who sold Bilberry Hill to the council in 1913. Neighbouring Cofton Hill (a continuation of Bilberry Hill) and Lickey Warren woods were purchased seven years later from his Hewell Estates. Now, the country park is managed for its conservation interest alongside its forestry

operations. Fire is always a problem, and you will notice the circular concrete pools along the summit ridge, supplied with water pumped from the river Arrow.

Turn south from the visitor centre and you are on the nature trails. Blue footprints mark the short walk, yellow the longer trail. Lickey is rich in birdlife in spite of its closeness to the city. Pines and larches attract siskins and redpolls in winter, and in irruption years, crossbills give their metallic calls from the canopy. Beneath the pines there is no vegetation so ground-nesting birds are absent. However, redstarts flirt orange tails here in spring as they bring food to young calling from nest-holes in the pines and nuthatches whistle loudly as they defy gravity on the trunks.

Below Cofton Hill is Lickey Warren, a flat pebble-strewn woodland criss-crossed with footpaths. Beech, sweet chestnut and oak grow here with an understorey of holly and hazel. The less acid soils encourage a wider range of plants including broad-leaved helleborine orchids and the rare lemon-scented fern. Coppicing is being reinstated here to encourage woodland flowers and to provide a ready source of hazel wands which make excellent walking sticks.

Beacon Hill

OSL Map 139
GR SO 987/759

OSP SO 87/97

*Access from B4096 at Red-
nal, south of Birmingham
or also Beacon Lane from
Rubery.*

*BCC: Grassland, birch-
woods and conifer planta-
tion. Superb views across
the suburbs of Birmingham
and the West Midlands.
Ideal for kite-flying and picnics. Paths good, but steep
gradients in places. Wheelchair access limited to hilltop grassland.*

*Public Transport: Bus from
Birmingham and Broms-
grove to Rednal and
Rubery.*

If you want uninterrupted views,
grassy picnic sites and pleasant
walks, Beacon Hill makes an ideal
venue. Just half a mile from the
Bilberry Hill centre, it is marked
from the Old Bromsgrove road.
En route to the car park in Monument Lane is the Lickey monument, an imposing 90 foot
obelisk erected in 1834 to the
memory of the fifth Earl of Plymouth by officers of Worcestershire Yeomanry cavalry.

Suburbia intrudes along Monu-

ment Lane, but the houses soon
give way to reveal the open space
of Beacon Hill. Beyond a flat
patch of rabbit-nibbled turf the
scarp suddenly drops away to a
golf course and the town of Rubery. To the west is the M5 motorway and the dark tuft of Frankley Beeches, a landmark for miles
around. Swifts careen along the
hillside below you in summer; in
winter the buffeting breezes are
literally uplifting. For all its urban
environment, it's an exhilarating
place.

South of the beacon and toposcope is an undulating walk between groves of conifers and
rhododendrons. The plant life is
less varied than that of Bilberry
Hill, for here you are on the Clent
Breccia, that red nutrient-poor
marl covering much of these
northern hills. Heather will not
grow in it, but broom burns gold
in May and the turf is starred with
heath bedstraw, luminously white
in summer.Bracken is abundant
and was once the basis of an industry here and at Clent. Huge
bundles were burnt to obtain
potash, which was moulded into
spheres known as "ess-balls" and
sold as a primitive soap in the
Black Country. Larches, lodgepole pines and western hemlock
are grown commercially to provide timber for the council
sawmill. Fencing, picnic tables
and park seats for the city of

Birmingham all have their origins in the Lickeys.

Pleasant though the hills are by day, they can present a different face by night. Then, according to legend, you may encounter the Devil and his huntsman Harry-ca-nab, mounted on white bulls seeking wild boar along the hilltops. Strange calls in the heavens are the sound of the Seven Whistlers, six birds of fate striving to find a seventh companion; when they do, it is said that the world will end.

Western Hills and Valleys

The traditional Worcestershire landscape is seen at its best in this unusually well-wooded part of the county. The rivers Teme and Severn thread through a fertile patchwork of fields and surprisingly extensive woodlands. Hopyards, cherry orchards and lush dingle woods characterise the Teme valley, while to the west is the Wyre Forest, rich in wildlife and largely unexplored.

Wassell Wood

Habberley Valley

Devil's Spittleful

Eyemore Wood and Trimpley Reservoir

The Wyre Forest
Callow Hill
Town Coppice and Hitterhill
Hawkbatch and Seckley Wood
Pound Green Common

Abberley Hill

Menith Wood

Rock Coppice

Ankerdine Common

Wassell Wood

OSL Map 138
GR S0 793/773

OSP SO 67/77

Access on minor road from Catchens End, Bewdley.

Woodland Trust. Steep deciduous woodland with numerous paths. Muddy in wet weather, and poorly-surfaced. Rich in wildlife with views across Severn valley.

Public transport: Bus to Bewdley from Kidderminster.

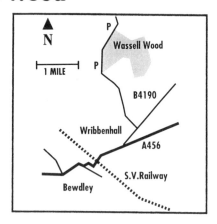

From Catchems End near Bewdley, an unpromising suburban road snakes gradually upwards between steep hedges, finally squeezing through a sandstone cutting to border a wood. This is Wassell Wood and it overlooks one of the finest landscapes in the county. To the west is the Severn valley, to the east the heathy countryside surrounding Kidderminster.

A welcoming Woodland Trust sign on the right-hand gatepost indicates general access and the salvation of the wood, for Wassell has been rescued at the eleventh hour. Destined for development as a caravan site and denuded of its finest oaks, it still bears the scars of previous plantings.

A circular route has been opened up through the trees, involving an initial climb parallel to the lane. This doubles as a bridle path so be prepared for mud in winter. Many introduced trees flourish in the wood, not least the sycamore, bane of conservationists. A vigorous alien first reliably documented in England in 1578, its broad leaves shade out competing native trees and compound their felony by rotting very slowly. As a result, plant life beneath sycamores is restricted to early-blossoming species which grab the available light while they can. Spring is the best season in which to enjoy the wood when primroses and bluebells are in bloom.

Red marl underfoot can make progress a little slippery as the path climbs to within sight of the wood's northern entrance. Turn right here uphill, and climb a stile into a newly-cleared area, once the site of a hill fort. Dark and sombre yews have been retained as befits their native status. Woodmen traditionally spare yews, possibly because the action brings luck, though a more prosaic explanation may lie in the extreme hardness of yew timber.

Views from this point are spectacular; to the north is Wolverley and beyond the western fringe of the Black Country. Small-leaved lime trees testify to the ancient nature of the surrounding countryside - there are few remaining in Wassell Wood itself.

Over a second stile the route offers a choice - right to retrace your steps or left to descend to the woodland bottom. On mild spring evenings after rain, the song of blackbirds is a delicious experience resonating against the wooded hill behind you and stretching out across the countryside to Bewdley and beyond . The solitude and views are well worth the gentle climb back to your starting place. For connoisseurs of woodland walks, Wassell is hard to beat. Spare a thought though, for the Woodland Trust and its volunteers faced with all those sycamores to clear!

Habberley Valley

OSL Map 138
GR SO 805/767

OSR SO 87/97

Access from B4190 Franche to Bewdley Road

WFDC: Lowland heather with oak and birch woodland - impressive sandstone outcrops. Ideal for picnics and short walks. Path sandy and good at all seasons.

Public Transport: Bus from Kidderminster to Bewdley, alight at Catchens End.

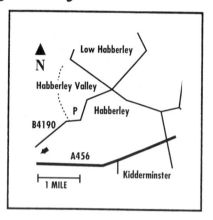

If it were not for the less-than-welcoming "Private Road" sign, travellers on the B4190 between Franche and Bewdley would miss Habberley completely. Concealed in the folds of countryside bordering north-west Kidderminster, the valley is a precious remnant of the heaths which once covered this corner of Worcestershire.

As you drive south from Franche, the road slices through a sandstone cutting and dips steeply into a natural bowl. At the bottom, on the right is a sandy track leading into the valley. It begins quietly, a crumbling metalled road between dry fields and copses of oak and birch. After a few minute's walk, you emerge into an open grassy heath - the perfect picnic spot.

Cars are a customary but unwelcome intrusion here. Residents have a right of vehicular access, but Wyre Forest District Council who purchased the valley in 1990, plan to ban cars and similar vehicles to non-residents. Earlier this century, charabancs packed with Black Country trippers brought valuable customers to Jennings' ice-cream shop.

Sepia postcards from the period portray a very different landscape. Huge lumps of sandstone rise above the heather and bracken and there a few trees of any size. The huge mass of Pecket Rock once stood proud, the focal point, but now barely breasts the treetops. Its friable surface is worn and grooved by clambering feet and proves irresistible to graffitists who have autographed every inch with carved initials.

As you follow the winding paths into the bracken and birch, the valley's most spectacular feature comes into view. A massive wall of sandstone over sixty feet high confronts you, an impassable barrier. Like the exposed rocks of the surrounding woodland it is a stubborn survivor of a searing red desert, transported here by scorching winds nearly 200 million years ago. The rock is a compacted sand dune, each of its grains polished by wind action. Softer surrounding deposits have been eroded by wind and water, leaving ridges of the harder Bridgnorth Sandstone in their wake.

Wildlife in this natural amphitheatre is typical of acid heath and, in common with the scenery, would benefit from drastic tree clearance. Heather now grows only along unshaded paths. Under the trees, bracken dominates, growing through a carpet of wavy hair grass. One attractive plant is white fumitory, a slender scrambling annual with creamy flowers and a cloud of feathery leaves. In early spring, slow-worms bask on beds of dried fern. These legless lizards are uniformly clay-brown and, unlike snakes have eyelids so that they can blink. Try to catch one and you could be left holding a writhing tail while the reptile makes its escape. A long list of birds includes nuthatch, tree pipit and spotted flycatcher. By far the most distinctive is the green woodpecker which announces its presence in spring with a maniacal laugh. As it flies up from its feeding site on a heathland anthill, the red crown and yellow rump look positively tropical, leading to reports of escaped parrots from inexperienced observers.

The sandstone wall creates a cul-de-sac leaving walkers with little option but to return by their outward route. Wassell Wood looms to the south and makes an interesting complementary site to visit. Alternatively, if you are hooked on heathland, try The Devil's Spittleful, just one mile away.

Devil's Spittleful

OSL Map 138
GR SO 807/759

OSP S087/97

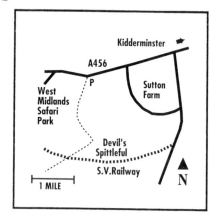

Access from A456 between Kidderminster and Bewdley, alongside entrance to West Midlands Safari Park.

Private/WFDC. Managed to WNCT. Acres of bowland heath.

Many sandy tracks through heather and birchwoods. Good paths and picnic areas. Severn valley Railway crosses site.

Public Transport: Bus along A456 from Kidderminster to Bewdley.

Few, if any other county places can offer you the chance to meet a baboon face to face. Nowhere else can you enjoy the song of willow warblers competing with a backcloth of roaring lions. This wild tract of heath on the very fringes of Kidderminster has more than a few surprises in store, steam trains included.

The chance of encountering a baboon or any primate is admittedly very slender. Once or twice they have escaped from the neighbouring West Midlands Safari Park, causing great excitement in the adjoining scout camp at Rhydd Covert, but occurrences are fortunately rare. Trains are much more regular now that the Severn Valley Railway operates from Kidderminster.

Like Habberley Valley, this is a sheltered spot, known well by locals, but impossible to see from a public road. The most convenient access point is from the A456 where a bridleway runs alongside the safari park entrance. Parking is limited, but there always seems to be room.

For about half a mile the sandy path is compressed between the privately owned Rhydd Covert and the safari park. Eventually it descends into a heathery plain dotted with clumps of gorse and broom and there is suddenly a wide choice of routes. To the right is the Spittleful or Spadeful itself, a sandstone outcrop crowned with Scots pines. No other tree is such an effective foil to the red rock as this, and on a cold sunny winter's afternoon, the sand glows against a backcloth of bottle-green.

In late summer and autumn, parasol mushrooms burst through the light soil and are well worth trying. Their enormous flaky brown caps are a complete meal and are delicious on toast with crisped bacon. Fungi are a speciality of the sand and the large reserve list includes the familiar and hallucinogenic fly agaric with white-spotted red caps and the dull brown roll-rim, which as its name suggests, has a turned-under cap with felted margins. It is deadly poisonous and should be avoided at all costs.

Parasol Mushrooms

47

The poor heathland terrain favours heather growth, but heather is soon crowded out by invading birch and hawthorn scrub. Don't be surprised if you see a work party of rangers and volunteers demolishing the bushes. Far from being vandals, they are trying to preserve the delicate balance between bare heath and birch woodland. Some areas, especially those near the railway tunnel, are regularly burnt to keep the heather fresh and young. These patches sprout anew within a few months and are home to a rare plant, the grey hair grass which forms spiky blue-green cushions on uncolonised ground.

Birdwatchers strolling around the Spittleful should notch up forty species with little effort on a summer's day. Tree pipits launch themselves from bushes and long-tailed tits build nests of feathers and lichen in the gorse thickets. Very occasionally a great grey shrike appears to quicken the pulse of both small birds, on which it preys, and ornithologists alike.

Paths are good throughout so there is little danger of getting lost. If you wish to explore further, cross the railway tunnel and climb onto the Rifle Range, an old barracks. Although this area is sandwiched uncomfortably between Stourport and Kidderminster, it is valuable heath but is inevitably under threat from development as golf course, tip or for mineral extraction. How long it survives depends on its significance as a local recreation area-the more people who use it the better.

Eymore Wood and Trimpley Reservoir

OSL Map 138
GR SO 775/793

OSP SO 67/77

On no-through road from Trimpley village.

Private/STWA. Oak woodland, conifer plantations and reservoir. River-bank paths along the Severn. Paths to good to rough, occasionally steep, muddy in wet weather. Views along Severn valley to Wyre Forest.

Public Transport: Nearest bus route from Kidderminster to Bewdley, 2 miles down river.

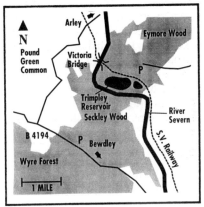

Waterside walks are rare in Worcestershire - this a lush, but well-drained county with scarcely any natural standing water. So, this area is doubly welcome, combining a reservoir fringe with outstanding scenery and a Severnside stroll.

To reach it, take the minor road west from Franche island, Kidderminster through the village of Low Habberley and up onto Jacob's Ladder the sandstone cliff that flanks Habberley Valley. At the top turn right towards Trimpley and first left, following the signposts, to Eymore Wood. This

descent into the valley is one of the finest views in Worcestershire, from which you can see most of the Wyre Forest and the Shropshire Clees beyond. A brief halt before you are swallowed up by the trees will often reveal a kestrel or buzzard soaring high over the woods.

A car-park and picnic area marks the end of the road. Here are signboards erected by HWCS and Severn Trent Water describing the Worcestershire Way (which zig-zags through Eymore Wood) and the reservoir respectively. The surrounding woodland is owned by the Arley Estate which has a refreshingly tolerant attitude to walkers; even if you stray off the paths, you are unlikely to be challenged, but do remember that this is private property. Polite notices request that horses keep to bridleways to minimise erosion.

From the car-park, there is a choice of paths and the one described here is for first-timers. Before you plunge down the wide ride to the water, just visible through the trees, take time to wander in the airy oakwood next to the road. In spring, they are excellent for birdwatchers. All three of our native woodpeckers live here along with nuthatches, marsh tits, treecreepers and , the stars of the show, pied flycatchers, a reminder that these woods are part of the Wyre Forest.

Follow any of the paths down to the bottom of the woods and you are naturally channelled towards a gateway across the Severn Valley railway line. If you have dogs or children, the usual precautions about safety apply, though the approach of a steam locomotive is anything but silent. Signs on the reservoir side beg you to take care of back-casters, fly-fishermen whose hooks may snag in clothing.

There are two reservoirs, built in the 1960s to supplement the Elan Valley water supply to Birmingham. No-one could say that they fit snugly into their surroundings, but their presence and the associated water treatment works has allowed walkers to gain access to

Cormorant

50

this section of the valley. And not just walkers - Trimpley has its own sailing and angling clubs and the sight of a flotilla of boats on a weekend afternoon is one to be enjoyed.

Other creatures appreciate the open water. Birds using the Severn as a migratory aid find welcome refuge on its surface and more welcome food beneath. Not all the hunched shapes around the banks in the mist of an autumn day are human anglers - some are grey herons. Very occasionally the valley is graced by a more spectacular visitor, a migrating osprey en route from breeding grounds in Scotland to winter quarters in the Mediterranean. For all their rarity, these are fearless birds and to see one take a trout in a slanting dive among the sails of yachts is an unforgettable experience. Don't be surprised to see the dark shape of a cormorant flapping wearily upriver; incongruous as these marine birds seem against the oakwoods of Wyre, they now occur all year round, commuting between Trimpley and Chelmarsh Reservoirs near Bridgnorth.

Most walkers leave the reservoirs' stony banks for the Severn rippling below. Here the river is not

The Wyre Forest

This, the county's largest block of woodland, is one of England's finest lowland oakwoods. Its survival, just twenty miles from Birmingham, is almost miraculous and even today, visitors rarely penetrate its deeper recesses. The A456 west of Bewdley skirts the forest warily and few minor roads intrude into its heartland. This is perhaps the only part of Worcestershire where you will feel like a genuine explorer. It's still possible to walk five miles from the centre and stay under trees all the way, though not necessarily in the county. Although the forest is always associated with Worcestershire - the words have an alliterative ring - half of its acreage is in Shropshire. The county boundary runs along the Dowles Brook, the archetypal forest stream, cold, clear and trout-filled, which bisects the woodland.

King John and the oak have ensured the forest's existence. In post-Conquest years it was enclosed as a royal hunting ground. Plantagenet and Tudor monarchs rode through the glades, questing for wild boar, deer and grouse. For centuries, Bewdley lived off the forest and its industry based on the oak tree. Oak was grown for timber, for underwood and for charcoal. Its bark is rich in tannin and had a ready market for curing leather at the Bewdley tannery. Now the oaks have been replaced in part by fast-growing conifers introduced by the Forestry Commission, but the identity of Wyre persists, encouraged by English Nature who own over 1,000 acres of coppice and manage them for wildlife.

East meets west in Wyre; north rubs shoulders with south. The pedunculate oaks of lowland Britain meet the sessile oaks of the Welsh hills. Bloody cranesbill and mountain melick grass, both hardy northerners, grow here alongside southern orchids. To savour the richness of the forest, you need to come regularly and explore it in depth. Here are three suggested access points to help you make a start.

Callow Hill

OSL Map 138
GR SO 751/740

OSP S0 67/77

On the A456 at Callow Hill, west of Bewdley

FC Conifer and oak woods with wide rides and four trails. Many flat paths suitable for wheelchairs. Visitor centre with displays, refreshments and toilets. Ample car parking.

Public Transport: Bus service from Bewdley to Ludlow along A456.

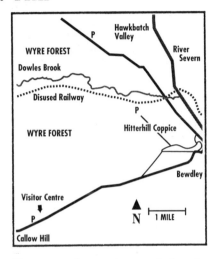

The first-time visitor to the Wyre Forest can do no better than begin at the Forestry Commission information centre at Callow Hill. It is signposted off the A456 west of Bewdley, about a mile and a half from the town centre and has ample parking (at a nominal, but unnecessary price). The interpretation centre is free though, and well-furnished with superb photographs and fascinating facts about the forest. Its showpiece is a wood ant nest, a timely reminder that you should always wear stout shoes in Wyre. Wood ants are everywhere and administer a painful bite to anyone rash enough to expose bare flesh to them.

There are four colour-coded trails leading from the car-park, varying in length from 1.5 to 5 kilometres. All are on sound paths and, for the most part wheelchair friendly, though in wet weather there are a few sticky patches. It's a good idea to keep to the paths (though you are free to wander at large on the Forestry Commission land) because the woodscape can be remarkably confusing and there are few landmarks.

Elsewhere there are more conifers; larch, Norway spruce and the impossibly straight lodgepole pine whose top-heavy crown is a liability in winds. Their severity is softened by regenerating birch and oak and the delicate flowers which grow along the forest rides. One of the most attractive is wood spurge, vivid lime-green in flower with red-flushed leaves in early spring.

As you wander along the green trail, you may notice a plaque drawing attention to the "Sorb Tree". No account of Wyre is complete without a potted history of this arboreal enigma. Also known as the "Whitty Pear", this European relative of the rowan was first publicised in 1678, when Edmund Pitts of Worcester, an apothecary and botanist wrote of "a rarity growing wild in a forest near Worcester". Cuttings were taken and two young trees raised in the Earl of Mountnorris' nursery at Arley Castle. No-one, not even the learned Edwin Lees of the Worcestershire Naturalists' Club, could explain the origins of the tree, known from nowhere else in Britain, though he may have come near in suggesting that the seed was brought from Aquitaine and planted in the garden of a hermitage. The cuttings were invaluable, because the parent tree was burnt down in 1862 by a poacher seeking revenge on the squire of Kinlet.

The tree you now see is a direct descendant of those cuttings and was planted in 1913. It has a cousin in the close of Worcester Cathedral, and recently another has been found in a wood in the south of the county - maybe there is more to discover about the absorbing sorb.

Tread quietly along the rides and you are likely to see fallow deer.

About three hundred now live in Wyre, not the descendants of the royal forest, but escapes from private parkland at Mawley, near Cleobury Mortimer in the 1890s. You first become aware of their presence by a skittering sound among the distant oaks, of insubstantial presences among the trunks. They rarely allow a close approach, melting into the trees like wraiths, superbly camouflaged against the russet winter leaves. They have reason to be wary; deer culls from the wooden hides are a necessary feature of forest management. The deer-lawns where fallows rut in autumn are distinguished by their open, trampled appearance, pitted with hoof-prints or slots. Many of the Wyre fallows are dark-coated, but all have the characteristic white spotted flanks in summer.

If you follow the trails deep enough in the forest, you eventually reach the disused railway line which once connected Bewdley and Cleobury Mortimer. Opened in 1861, it fell beneath the Beeching axe exactly a hundred years later and is now being reclaimed by heather and dog-roses. The longest (red) trail includes a short stretch of the line, before heading north once again into the beech and conifer groves. Just where it leaves the line grow a few wild columbines, deep blue-purple and less showy than their garden relatives - hunt them down in June, but leave them for others to enjoy.

Town Coppice and Hitterhill

OSL Map 138
GR SO 772/763

OSP S0 67/77

Access along Dry Mill Lane from A456 at Bewdley.

English Nature/Private. Ancient oak coppice with chain of pools and disused railway line. Woodland brook and old orchard. Rich in wildlife with good and flat paths. Wheelchair access along metalled section of railway line.

Public Transport: Bus service to Bewdley from Thummingshow and Kidderminster.

English Nature acquired over 50 acres of ancient oak coppice at Hitterhill in 1992 and all are open to the public. This walk through the area includes large sections of the National Nature Reserve and is one the best wildlife sites. The route is a recommendation only and you are generally free to wander at will.

The best access point is from Dry Mill Lane, Bewdley, an old forestry extraction route. To reach it, take the A456 out of Bewdley town and, after about half a mile, turn right at the Hop-pole Inn. Take the first right-hand fork of this narrow lane, and you will soon reach a small car-park on the left by the English Nature signboard. In August, the rose-pink flowers of keeled garlic can be seen below this sign. Turn left along the disused railway and immediately left again to follow a rutted forest path deep into the oaks. Lily-of-the-valley blooms on the trackside edges in May to be succeeded by yellow cow-wheat in high summer.

All the oaks here are sessile oaks, typical of western acid woods over poor soil. Their tall trunks rise above a woodland with virtually no shrub layer. Only bracken, bilberry and straggly heather can survive beneath the spreading oak canopy. Sessile oaks are distinguished from the pedunculate oak by their acorns which have no stalks or "peduncles". Many of the trees have been coppiced and show a pronounced kink at their base where they arise from the old stool. Up to the 1930s, coppicing was carried out here; the forest was divided into "falls",each cut on a 25 year rotation for mature timber and at lesser intervals for bean sticks, refinery poles for the Black Country iron foundries and pit-prop poles. Bark-peeling was a regular occupation for forest women who stripped green oak branches to supply Bewdley tannery.

Evidence of charcoal-burning can still be seen in places, a ring of ferny grass where the burners constructed their wooden turf-covered mounds. Air was restricted and the oak burned slowly over several days resulting in fine furnace charcoal. Throughout the wood are the dark umbrellas of yews, under which the burners stored their timber to keep it dry.

The path soon drops away to the right into a deep valley crossed by a footbridge. A surprise here is a deep pool covered with yellow fringed water-lilies and surrounded by rhododendrons. These bushes are rampant all along the stream and, though they were introduced by a past landowner for decorative effect, have now blotted their copybook. No doubt their removal will be a priority for English Nature.

The path along the stream leads north past other pools, now silting up, through open oak woodland. In late summer it can appear empty, save for the odd fallow deer or grey squirrel, but in spring this coppice is alive with birdsong. Wood warblers, real high-forest songsters trill from the oaks, shivering from beak to tail with the effort of song. Blue and great tits are everywhere, feeding youngsters in nest-boxes and tree-crannies. And, high over the treetops, sparrowhawks wheel in territorial display.

Down in the moss and leaflitter at the base of old oaks lurks a rare insect, the land caddis. It is the only terrestrial member of its fam-

ily, the larva constructing a case of sand-grains to protect its soft body. Land caddises are almost confined to Wyre in the whole of Britain and were discovered here by the local naturalist and author, Norman Hickin. Look for the tiny cigar-shaped case among dead oak-leaves in spring and summer. When you reach the top of the stream valley, turn right along a driveway lined with Douglas firs planted in the 1870s. This path borders a cleared area called Ruskin Land and was indeed named after the Victorian poet and moralist. Ruskin formed a band of like-minded people- the Guild of St. George- to practise his principles of equality and just payment and the land here was donated by George Baker, former mayor of Birmingham.

Past Ruskin Land, the path forks to the right through dense oak coppice to another pool and beyond a superb old orchard, dotted with anthills. Wild thyme and yellow tormentil adorn these ancient hummocks and redstarts flash orange in the old plum trees. The path crosses a bridge over the old railway line to Lodge Hill Farm, the home of English Nature's warden for Wyre. In July orange silver-washed fritillaries crowd the thistle heads; their almost identical relatives,the high brown fritillaries have virtually disappeared from the forest as from much of lowland Britain.

One insect to watch out for is the hornet. Now scarce in Worcestershire, it nests in hollow trees and can be identified by sheer size, not to mention its wasp-like shape and dusting of fox-brown hair. If you find a nest, don't stand in the flight-line of commuting adults-you have been warned!

Another potential problem can be seen along the railway cutting which takes you back to your starting place. Adders bask on the rocky banks and can occasionally be seen coiled and motionless, especially in spring when they emerge from a communal hibernaculum. These snakes are fairly common in Wyre but not often seen - they usually disappear long before you see them. Dr.Sylvia Sheldon of Knowles Mill has studied the adders of the forest and can now recognise up to 250 individuals which she has marked. The very few people who have received adder bites have either stepped on one or placed their hands on a snake as they scramble up a bank. If you see one, ad-mire it from a distance and keep its location to yourself.

A short distance along the metalled line sees you at your car again. As an added diversion turn left along Dry mill Lane and you come to Dowles Brook. Dulas is Celtic for dark and dark this stream is, running swiftly over polished sandstone past shingle beaches. In the Fred Dale reserve owned jointly by the WNCT and WMBC you can see dippers. grey wagtails and kingfishers along the brookline. Beneath the stones a few crayfish hide, although their numbers are now much reduced by disease. Bullheads are common as well as fingerling trout, which dart beneath the overhanging alder roots. If you want to explore Dowles in depth, cross the bridge into Shropshire and follow the forest road to Cooper's Mill, you won't be disappointed.

Adder

Hawkbatch and Seckley Wood

OSL Map 138
GR SO 761/777 (car park)

OSP S0 67/77

On B4194 north-west of Bewdley.

FC. Conifer plantation and oak woodland with views across the Severn Valley to Trimpley. Many good paths and three trails. Wheelchair access along trails.

Public Transport: Bus service from Bewdley to Cleobury Mortimer, alight at Buttonoak.

Travel north-west from Bewdley on the Buttonoak road and you enter the forest shortly after crossing the Dowles Brook. Hawkbatch plantation lies about a mile on to your right, signposted by the Forestry Commission. Picnic tables and a choice of woodland walks, colour-marked for length, await you.

The shortest (white) route is a flat and uninspiring stroll through thick scrub, a mass of regenerating birch, oak and rowan thrusting among Scots and Corsican pine. Eventually, after a mile-long meander, it deposits walkers back where they started, having offered no views and little wildlife.

Take the red or the green paths, however and you will obtain stunning views across the Severn valley. First though, another word about wood ants.

Here, among the conifers, they are everywhere. In spring they emerge in the first suspicion of sunlight and cluster together in dark, seething masses. Then, they are relatively sluggish, but in high summer become disturbingly active, streaming over paths and ascending tall trees. The nests of conifer needles and leaf litter are impressive mounds, usually aligned with a southern aspect to catch the sun. Wood ant bites are painful - they are insect Rottweilers - and take some time to remove. Peer over a nest and the workers squirt formic acid at you; put out your tongue and you can taste the sharp spots of liquid, but be sure to check that no-one else is around. Hold a bluebell or harebell over the nest and it will change from blue to pink as sure as litmus.

Large and showy flowers have no place in Wyre; the accent is on beauty in miniature. As you reach the route of the Elan Valley aqueduct, a broad swathe of grass between the trees, tiny eyebrights and milkwort glow among the turf. Meadow brown and gatekeeper butterflies mingle with the woodland species such as speck-

58

led wood. Follow the red trail and you soon reach the Severn lookout. On the edge of a steep sandstone cliff, oaks have been cleared to create a superb view of Trimpley Reservoir below. Landslips are frequent along this forest fringe, where pockets of clay moistened by rain, bring down tons of sandstone in a tangle of roots and rock. On blustery winter days you can often see herons, blown upriver by the gales, like airborne mackintoshes. The steam trains of the Severn Valley railway can always be heard in summer.

Signposts on the red trail direct you to the Seckley Beech, a venerable and famous tree on the edge of the slope. Alas, this natural monument, once known as the 32-trunk tree, has been felled for safety reasons and its grey limbs sprawl across the floor like an octopus in rigor mortis. Many names are carved into its bark, see if you can find an earlier date than 1930, our best effort.

Pound Green Common

OSL Map 138
GR SO 753/788

OSP SO 67/77

Along minor road to Arley from B4194 at Buttonoak.

Private Common. Wooded common with bracken and birch. Good views of Wyre Forest. Many good and flat paths but difficult to penetrate in mid-summer before the bracken is cut.

Public Transport: Bus from Bewdley to Cleobury Mortimer. Alight at Buttonoak.

Enclosed by a pincer movement of the Wyre Forest, Pound Green lies hard against the Shropshire boundary. Drive along the Buttonoak road from Bewdley and take the first turn left to Arley. Few people notice the common, which is screened by small fields and old orchards. If you want to see it before it vanishes beneath a tide of oaks, birch and bracken, go soon.

Many ungrazed commons in Worcestershire are losing their character as commoners' rights are left unexercised. Here the taking of bracken and grazing of ducks, geese and poultry is registered. Once, foresters could lay claim to land on the common if they built a house - usually a chimney - and had smoke rising from it within 24 hours. Not everyone managed this difficult task and one such failed attempt, the "Hovel Orchard" is known to this day.

The common is best reached from a footpath alongside a boarding kennels. The overriding impression is of a sea of bracken punctuated by birch and oak saplings. Only if paths have been cut will you glimpse remnants of the common's previous incarnation; glowing cushions of magenta bell heather and sky-blue harebells edging the route. Lizards are regularly seen sunning themselves on dry tuffets of thyme and the funnel-shaped webs of the labyrinth spider can be found on dry banks.

The birds are those typical of lowland heath-tree pipits, yellowhammers, whitethroats and green woodpeckers. Cuckoos call in spring. Pound Green was the study area of Edgar Chance who first studied the odd breeding habits of the cuckoo, later publishing his findings in his book "The Cuckoo's Secret"

Having explored the common, you may wish to visit Arley station along the lane, now owned by the Severn Valley Railway and magnificently kept.

Lesser Spotted Woodpecker

60

Abberley Hill

OSL Map 138
GR SO 750/674 (access from Worcestershire Way)

OSP SO 66/76

On minor road from B4202 north of Great Witley.

Private: Plantation and deciduous woodland over limestone. Large quarry at eastern end. Paths variable, but slippery in wet weather and muddy at most times. Some steep sections.

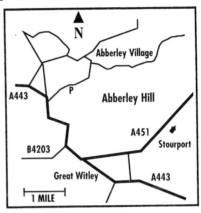

Abberley Hill is one of north Worcestershire's most familiar landmarks. To travellers from the east it is the first high ground you can see, sharing the honour with the conifered crown of Woodbury Hill. Both are outposts of the Malvern Axis, a ridge of Silurian limestone stretching north from the Malvern Hills, fifteen miles to the south. Trees now cover its sharply angled summit which curves protectively around Abberley village. Although it is only 870 feet high, this is an impressive hill, well worth climbing for the wide-ranging views. Walkers along the Worcestershire Way have to ascend gradually, but you can take a short-cut to the top. From the Hundred House hotel at Great Witley, drive up the B4202 and turn first right at the top. This narrow and very steep lane lies on the Worcestershire Way route and offers limited parking. On the right after a few hundred yards is a HWCS signpost and waymarker indicating the path and a suggested circular walk to include Abberley village.

The first burst of walking is unexciting, a plod beneath dull sycamores. Conifers are often branded as killers of woodland flora, but, as you can see here, sycamores are equally destructive. Apart from the shuttlecocks of broad buckler ferns, there is virtually no ground vegetation. The soil has a lot to do with the sparse cover, for here it is red breccia, the same marly mix that covers Clent.

Soon you emerge at the triangulation point and views to the south open up before you. Paramount above all landmarks is the ornate clock-tower in the grounds of Abberley House, now an exclusive school for boys. Built in 1883 by cotton magnate Joseph Jones, it is 161 feet high and was constructed by the industrialist to overlook the land of his neighbour, the Earl of Dudley at Witley Court. Beyond the tower are the hills of the Teme valley decorated by a wide ribbon of dingle woodland. The famous Shelsley Walsh hill climb course which stages regular events in summer, can just be made out snaking among the trees.

Trees have claimed most of Abberley and open spaces are few. Patches of grassland are there to be found if you look hard and have a legacy of herbs. Wild thyme still hangs on in rabbit-nibbled turf and is complemented by sprigs of wild basil in late summer. Don't bring the kite, though- the trees soon re-appear and the paths become dark and mysterious. There is more or less continuous cover as you proceed along the ridge, now dipping into tunnels of blackthorn and elder, now climbing past old yews, relics of the primary woodland which once graced Abberley.

Here and there open stands of bracken allow light to penetrate and you may see flocks of foraging tits, nuthatches and treecreepers in the undergrowth. Most of this woodland has been planted - sweet chestnut for its long, straight poles, ideal for fencing, and sycamores for their clean, white timber, once used to make piano keys. Conifers are here too,

mainly Norway spruce, the familiar Christmas tree, and larch.

The muddy and slippery bridleway keeps to the crown of the hill for most of its length, but the Worcestershire Way veers eastwards and drops towards Yarhampton. You can continue along the ridge if you prefer, but soon the large quarry becomes a natural barrier and the abrupt descent at Shaver's End is not for the cautious. The Worcestershire Way leaves the cover of the trees to clip the corner of a cornfield. Look to the south-east with the hill on your right and there is a splendid view of Witley Court with Malvern's North Hill rising behind it. Witley Court was built in Italianate style in 1860 by the first Earl of Dudley. Victorian royalty and aristocracy were regular visitors to its grandiose chambers where entertainment of lavish proportions took place sumptuously and often. In 1937, after the house had been purchased by Sir Herbert Smith, a Kidderminster blanket millionaire, a disastrous fire broke out.

Witley Court was burnt and looted, its sheer scale preventing reconstruction. Now it survives as a gaunt ruin and though the huge Poseidon fountain no longer plays, it is an evocative place.

The most elegant part of the estate still remains: the neighbouring chapel has been described as "the finest baroque church in Britain". Ornately gilded and painted by Antonio Bellucci, its ceiling is magnificent - after your walk it makes an excellent venue.

The bridleway now skirts the lower edge of the limestone quarry which distinguishes Abberley to travellers from the east. Grey fossil-rich stone from this excavation is used primarily for road-building. A feast of blackberries grows along this bridleway, so remember to pack a container for them in season. There are over 200 species of blackberry in Britain, but not all taste good. One of the best, found here, is Rubus ulmifolius, the elm-leaved blackberry which can be identified by its pink flowers and pale undersides to the leaves. Its berries are tightly-bunched, firm and sweet, but take care not to pick them after September 30th when, according to legend, Old Nick jumps into them.

The bridleway joins the minor road at Shaver's End. Turn left and you can follow the quiet lane back to Abberley village. Another bridleway leads off this lane after a few hundred yards taking you across arable land to Abberley by a different route.

Buzzard

Menith Wood

OSL Map 138
GR SO 705/693

OSP S0 66/76

Off minor road from A443, one mile west of Stockton-on-Teme

Private: Steep dingle woodland with mixture of conifer and native trees. Bridleways very muddy in wet weather and many paths steep. Excellent wood for exploring and for access to nearby Frith Common.

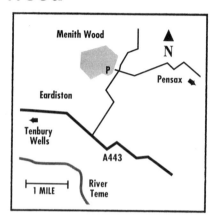

Having sampled some of Worcestershire's flatter woods, you are now ready to tackle the challenging contours of one of the county's finest. Menith Wood, perched high above the Teme valley on an outcrop of limestone, has it all. Even its name beckons with a primitive quality and more than a hint of foreboding; one false step in places here could mean your last!

However, don't let this deter you - there are good paths through the trees, but be prepared for a little breathlessness.

By car, the wood is best approached along a winding, uphill lane from the A443 between Stockton and Eardiston. In spring red earth contrasts with a haze of cherry blossom wreathing the many orchards for which the Teme is renowned. As the lane levels out, cottages mark the edge of the wood which is signposted to the left. Parking is very restricted, so take care to avoid blocking access to residents and woodland machinery.

A choice of routes offers a descending bridleway or a path over a stile through smooth-barked beeches, all planted for timber. The more interesting route follows the bridleway past a cottage and into an old orchard. Between the gnarled boughs of ancient cherries, the Teme valley stretches before you in a hundred shades of green. Red-tinged poplars, emerald larches and blackish pines make up a soft patchwork relieved here and there by the terracotta square of a freshly-ploughed field.

Follow the path down into the orchard, studded with what appear to be overgrown molehills. Topped with thyme. these tuffets are inviting seats, but resist the temptation to use them. They are the hills of yellow ants, many decades old and are a rare sight in agricultural England today.

Beneath a venerable pine, the bridleway re-enters the wood. In winter this section is churned chocolate by horses' hooves and you may be forced to teeter uncertainly at the edges. This stretch is short, soon joining a driveway to Dumbleton Farm. At its lowest point, the path crosses the Dumbleton Brook which bites deep into the soft limestone, gouging dingles for which the area is well-known. Progress along these is tempting but very hard going. Early in the year they offer tantalising glimpses of fern-strewn outcrops and green garlic spears, soon to be hidden by the summer's growth. It's easy here in the depths of the wood, to forget the outside world until the flash of a soaring sparrowhawk or the bubbling of a curlew tugs at your senses.

Where curlews call, coal was once mined. Menith marks the limits of the Forest of Wyre coalfield and drift mines were operative here until the 1940's. Known locally as "dilly-holes", these shallow walkdown mines exploited seams close to the surface and yielded a poor, sulphurous coal. There has since been pressure to re-open them, but such plans would be disruptive to say the least.

The bridleway strikes up through the wood passing exposures of ochre limestone. Botanically the wood is confusing since its geology allows lime-loving plants (calcicoles) to grow side-by-side with acid-loving species (calcifuges). So, here we have heather rubbing roots with sanicle, wood bittervetch with spurge laurel. This last, incidentally, is neither a spurge or a laurel, but a relative of the pink-flowered garden daphne. In winter it resembles a small rhododendron with waxen green blooms.

At the top of the path, houses mark the proximity of the lane and one right turn followed by another brings you to your starting point. However, the adventurous can turn left before the first house along a rough track between hazel coppice and a pine plantation. Before long the path narrows and the ground falls steeply away to your right. Primroses and bluebells grow on these vertiginous slopes above the stream, but they are completely safe from picking. How far you continue is a matter of choice - at the bottom is the bridlepath once more, so you will need to retrace your steps uphill.

Rock Coppice

OSL Map 138
GR SO 710/640

OSP SO 66/76

On minor road south from Stanford Bridge on the Teme.

Private: Lime and oak dingle woodland with some conifers and outcrop of tufa. Paths are steep and very muddy in the wood. Good walks along fields nearby and excellent views across Teme Valley.

Public Transport: MRW 310 312 313

The Teme valley woods are not really open spaces within the meaning of this book. They are, however, well served with public footpaths and are so beautiful, mysterious and unvisited that they are impossible to omit. Who,after all, could resist places with names like Devil's Den, Death's Dingle and Witchery Hole?

Rock Coppice is an excellent starting point. All you need is a good O/S map and a degree of persistence to find it. The approach is as good as the walk itself. The A451 road westwards from Great Witley plunges headlong towards the Teme into one of the most spectacular land-

scapes in the English Midlands. Immediately beyond Stanford Bridge is a left turning to Shelsley Walsh, famous for its hill climb. About half-a-mile along the minor road is a cluster of derelict barns roofed with corrugated iron. Parking is restricted but there is usually room for up to four cars at the laneside. Opposite the barns, a public footpath (unmarked by a signpost) leads through a tangle of bristling burdock and hogweed. After a hundred yards or so, you reach the cool shade of Rock Coppice. Boots are essential in all seasons since the path through the wood is steep and extremely wet in places. Poplars and spruces have been planted even on these slopes, but the ferny banks of the stream are untouched and bordered by limes and wych elm. In this quiet dingle is the essence of the Teme woodlands.

Slip-sliding uphill for a few minutes, you soon reach a fork in the path. To the left is the rock that gives the coppice its name. As high as a double-decker bus, Southstone Rock is a massive exposure of tufa or travertine, possibly the largest in England. It looks porous and crumbly like a gargantuan piece of bathroom pumice, but is a durable material formed when water-borne deposits of lime leach out from the underlying Psammosteus Limestone. Gardeners are especially fond of tufa as a substrate for alpines. At nearby Shelsley it has a more practical use. St.Andrew's church there is built from blocks of tufa and dates from the 12th century.

Follow the spring gurgling around the rock and you can see the tufa "factory" itself, a shelf of sodden emerald moss, held together by a lattice of lime - touch it and it "gives" like cake-icing! Children (and their parents) love to explore Southstone's fissures and crannies where clefts are just wide enough to admit a human body. However, great care is needed at the top where the brink is concealed by foliage - if you have children with you extra vigilance is required here. Remains of an old cottage still survive amidst a Rackhamesque riot of roots and rock.

After exploring the tufa, you can return to your original path and climb to the top of the wood where a waymarked bridlepath crosses the stream over a wooden bridge. This section is extremely muddy and can be something of a challenge in winter. Soon you emerge into open pasture with superb views of the valley across to Abberley Hill and its Victorian clock tower and the old hill fort at Woodbury, now swamped by a cloak of conifers. The hedge to your right is composed of small-leaved limes, a woodland "ghost" carved directly out of the wildwood.

Follow the hedgelines and the blue arrow signs to descend steeply into Devil's Den, a deep wooded dingle complete with rushing streamlet. Much of this wood has been destroyed by poplar plantings, but on its sloping sides oaks and ashes linger on. Note the soil change as you enter - bracken and broom are thriving here in the red sandy soil.

From here it's all downhill, a pleasant stroll to the lane. Look out for the coppiced limes by the path which have been attacked by sap-sucking woodpeckers. Neat diamond-shaped holes ring the bark where the birds have drunk their fill and then moved on.The path reaches the lane after crossing a small field and your starting-place is a few hundred yards to the left.

Ankerdine Common

OSL Map 150 GR SO 736/567

OSP SO 65/75

Along no-through road off B4197 at top of Ankerdine Hill.

HWCC. Picnic site with excellent views across Teme Valley. Steep walks into adjacent woods.

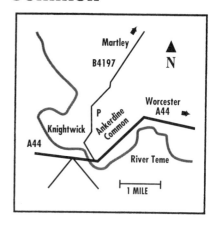

You need to be extra-vigilant to spot this tiny common which is also a picnic site developed and managed by HWCS. Even locals have difficulty in finding it, but its rewards far outweigh its diminutive size. To get there, take the B4197 south from Martley across the limestone ridge of the "Malvern Axis". As the road bends on the very brink of its plunge down Ankerdine Hill, keep straight on along a no-through road between houses. Soon you will see the familiar signboards and picnic tables of HWCS together with a small parking area. Here, over the sapling oaks and banks of willowherb, there are hints of the views for which the spot is renowned, but the best place is further along the lane. Walk for a few hundred yards along the gravelled path and you reach another picnic table set on a tiny patch of grass, encircled by oaks and brambles. Ahead the

Teme valley is laid before you, a patchwork of copses and fields, some in Worcestershire, but most in Herefordshire.

This secluded spot is the perfect place for a quiet and undisturbed picnic - take a bottle of wine and a hamper on a warm summer evening and watch the sun set over the Suckley Hills. It's the bucolic equivalent of a box at the theatre!

To the west the oast-houses at Whitbourne mark the beginning of hop-growing country. Hop-yards are still frequent in the sheltered Teme valley where the well-drained alluvial soil suits the plants. Unfortunately the threat of disease, the dreaded Verticillium "wilt", has taken its toll and some fields are now out of commission. Hops spring each year from a stout rootstock, and by August their trailing stems or bines will be approaching thirty feet in length. The bines are trained along wire frames criss-crossed with a network of twine for support. When the clusters of light-green cones reach maturity in early autumn, they are harvested by machine and dried in kilns.

Before the Second World War, hop-picking was entirely manual, providing a working holiday for many Black Country families. Trainloads from Dudley, Brierley Hill and Netherton set out each September to work in the Temeside yards: "as long as a hop-picking train" was a familiar Black Country expression.

People were recruited in the towns beforehand by experienced women and, having packed their "hopping-boxes", arrived to set up temporary homes in barns, caravans and outhouses. All human life was there - seasoned grandmothers, youths with thoughts of rowdy nights in Worcester, cultured folk who had fallen on hard times and a host of shadowy opportunists not seen from one season to the next. When the last hopyard ceased hand-picking in 1951, the Black Country lost a valuable link with its rural past.

From the picnic area, paths lead enticingly into the surrounding oakwoods. Many are steep, as Worcestershire Way walkers will confirm, but provide pleasant strolls through ancient woodland. Wild service trees can be found among the cherries and oaks, proof of antiquity should you need it, and in July you can search for the nettle-leaved bellflower, a showy blue campanula, often planted in gardens, but genuinely wild here.

Southern Hills and Commons

The Malverns dominate Worcestershire's south-western corner, towering abruptly from the Severn plain. Nearly thirty miles of footpath and the county's best views make them irresistible to walkers. Less well-known are the flat commons which surround the hills and which well repay exploration. The Severn estuary once stretched to Longdon, south-east of Malvern and its marshy legacy can still be detected in the post-drainage regularity of the field pattern and the pollard willows.

Malvern Hills
North Hill and Worcestershire Beacon
Pinnacle Hill
Chase End and Ragged Stone Hill

Castlemorton Common
Hollybed Common

Ravenshill Wood

Suckley Hills

The Knapp and Papermill

Old Hills Common

Marsh Common and Dunstall Common

Normoor Common
Ashmoor Common

Malvern Hills

"I will lift up mine eyes to the hills". That is the motto of Great Malvern town council and, to residents and visitors alike, it's advice that is difficult to ignore. This part of the county is dominated by the massive nine-mile ridge of the Malvern chain rising steeply and improbably from the lush Severn plain. These are the oldest rocks in England, buttresses of pre-Cambrian granite over 600 million years old. They are also the highest points in the county reaching 1394 feet on the Worcestershire Beacon directly above the town.

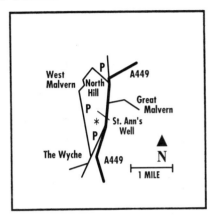

Once a Royal Forest, Malvern Chase occupied over 7,000 acres of field and woodland in medieval times when it extended into Herefordshire and Gloucestershire. Until the reign of Edward I. it was the hunting ground of kings, including King John, an indefatigable pursuer of all things furred and feathered, often preferring to follow his quarry on foot. The chase was presented to Gilbert de Clare on his marriage to Edward's daughter and until the 16th century underwent a series of ownerships. Henry VII regained royal possession, but in the reign of Charles I financial crises forced the king to sell in spite of the wishes of the commoners who occupied various portions of the forest. Eventually he quelled their riots by granting two-thirds of the

area to them and the chase was disafforested by decree in 1632. The common thus acquired includes the surviving tracts of Castlemorton Common. Link Common and Barnard's Green.

Increasing enclosure and encroachment by commoners led to the passing of an Act of Parliament, the Malvern Hills Act, to preserve the character of the hills. Under this act the Conservators were established and empowered to enact bye-laws, maintain roads and paths and to prevent excess mineral extraction. You will see evidence of their work everywhere on the hills, especially at car-parks (where they make a nominal charge) and in erosion-prone places. There is no doubt that the commons which make up much of the accessible land have benefited immeasurably from the work of the Conservators.

71

One of the best features of the Malverns is their ease of access. Corseted by roads, the larger hills are very well served by car-parks and walks to the summits are generally short, though you can make them as long as you like depending on where you begin. For the best introduction to the 30 miles or 50 of footpath, visit Malvern Tourist Information Centre which is crammed with suggested walks, facts and figures and details of access. They're not averse to name-dropping there either, though given the names associated with the area- Elgar, Shaw, Jenny Lind and John Masefield- you can hardly blame them.

North Hill and Worcestershire Beacon

OSL Map 150 GR Tank Quarry SO 771/469

OJP SO 64/74 GR Wyche Cutting SO 769/337

Off B4218, Wyche Cutting and B4232 West Malvern road. Access also from Great Malvern town centre - follow signs to the Anne's Well.

Open hilltop common with magnificent views across the whole of Worcester-shire. Walks, picnics and kite-flying.

Toilets at Wyche Cutting. Wheelchair access along Beach Lane from Wyche Cutting.

Public Transport: Buses from Worcester, Upton. Trains to Malvern Link and Barnard's Green.

These are the hills the summit-baggers climb. At 1394 feet, the Worcestershire Beacon is the highest point in the county, but makes a modest trophy by comparison with the whalebacks farther west. Nevertheless the views are incomparable and it is possible to win them with remarkably little effort.

You can climb the Beacon from Great Malvern town, but the easiest ascent is from the Wyche Cutting, an old salt road through the granite. From Great Malvern head south in the shadow of the hills and, after a mile or so turn right towards Colwall and the Wyche. At the top of the hill houses cling improbably to the bare rock, facing the Severn plain over 800 feet below. There is plenty of parking on the west side of the cutting, either by the roadside or preferably in the Conservators' car-park.

Take the north-bound track along Beacon Lane where the houses peter out after a few hundred yards. This is the summit road, metalled throughout. Although it lacks the appeal of a rocky path, it can be used by wheelchair-owners and walkers with unsuitable shoes. After a short distance, a circular stone marks the approximate whereabouts of a 220 feet deep mine excavated between 1711 and 1721. The Bristolian who sank the shaft was searching for gold rumoured to be here in small quantities, but his search proved fruitless and the hole has now been filled in.

The road continues along the spine of the hills, gaining height rapidly to reveal the Malvern straits stretching across to Bredon Hill to the east. Some anonymous observers with sharp eyes and sharper imaginations claim to have seen fifteen counties from the Beacon, though how many are visible since the boundary reshuffle is open to debate. You can only bid for a new total on a clear day, preferably in spring or autumn. Summer hazes and winter fogs restrict visibility considerably, but at any season the cool breezes or gusty winds are a contrast with the climate below. It's no surprise that Malvern is kite-flying country par excellence - the town has England's biggest and best kite shop.

A steady climb will soon bring you to the Beacon itself, girded with granite and surmounted by a toposcope indicating the direction of various landmarks. From here you can tick off the Shropshire Wrekin, the Clent Hills on the county's northern rim and the Cotswolds to the south. Manmade eminences include the Three Choirs cathedrals of Gloucester, Hereford and Worces-

ter, and the priories of Great and Little Malvern. To the immediate south the chain of hills stretches for seven miles of spectacular ridge-walking.

All of which assumes that there is a view at all. One of the thrills of walking the Malverns is to climb in an autumnal mist when the cloud-base drags across the tops and the grasses are beaded with dew. As the weather improves, the fog rolls back to expose the landscape piecemeal. In any season you will be grateful for the walled picnic area set among the spiky summit outcrops - once there was a cafe (hence the metalled road), but it was destroyed by fire several years ago and fortunately not rebuilt.

To the north of the Beacon, the ground drops away only to rise again to North Hill and Table Hill. The springy turf leading down to the saddle between the hills is shelter for many birds. Little brown jobs rising from almost underfoot are either meadow pipits or skylarks - the former flutter weakly around calling a thin "seep" while the larks flush with a liquid "chirrup". If you are very fortunate, you may see the dark cross of a peregrine hanging over the quarries on North Hill. Each year these dramatic falcons spend a few days in autumn harassing the local pigeons. More usually there are squadrons of kestrels hovering in the updrafts, family parties hunting in formation.

Wild flowers are few and far between on these poor soils, but foxgloves, gorse and rosebay willowherb are all common. Bilberries also thrive in enormous circular patches, turning red in October. The bilberry rings can be seen as glowing blood-red discs from Malvern Link .

To the east of the saddle along a descending path is St. Anne's Well. The Malvern waters have long been renowned for their purity, attracting a reputation for curative properties unsubstantiated by science. In Victorian times this was a popular social venue. The building is faced with the dour Malvern stone and has a pump-room where you can sample the waters.

To vary your return to the Wyche, you can follow the lower path to the west of the Beacon, parallel to the West Malvern road.

A longer and more demanding route to North Hill runs from The Tank Quarry car-park at North Malvern. This large excavation once provided rock for roads across the south of England, but is now derelict and colonised by buddleia. Follow the track north from the car-park, keeping right throughout. Soon you reach Ivy Scar Rock, the largest single outcrop on the hills.

Its surface is greasy with a lichen known as rock-tripe because, in spite of its appearance, it is edible. To the immediate right of the rock runs an ascending path called the Zig-Zags, for obvious reasons. As you climb, the town below is gradually revealed. Malvern Priory stands out, a magnificent construction housing one of the finest collections of stained glass in England. It was built between 1400 and 1460 on Norman Foundations. At the top of the Zig-Zags is a broad ride called Lady Howard de Walden's Drive, constructed for use of a coach and horses and ideal for a circuit of Sugarloaf Hill and Table Hill. To vary your return route and to dodge the mountain-bikes, descend down Green Valley through an avenue of sycamores. At the base of this steep valley, turn left to the north and regain the car-park after about fifteen minute's walk.

Inside the rock houses high on Vale Rock, Kingsford Country Park (page 16) just north of Kidderminster. Inhabited until 1961, they were once connected to gas and water services. Note the iron props supporting the roof, necessary since vandals have hewn the soft sandstone away.

The Forestry Commission's Visitor Centre at Callow Hill, Wyre Forest (page 53) near Bewdley. Inside are refreshments, information, publications, photographs, maps and... wood ants!

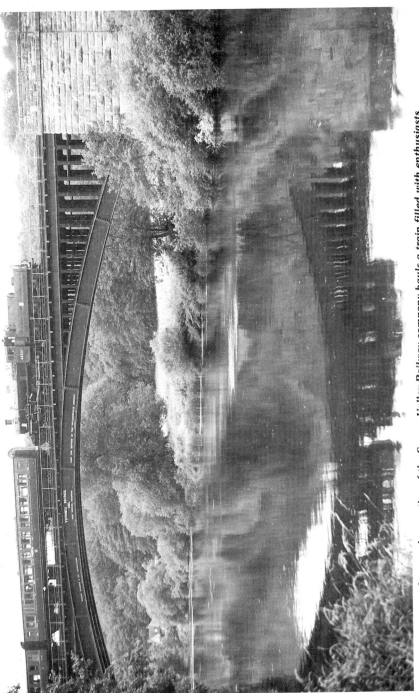

A steam locomotive of the Severn Valley Railway company hauls a train filled with enthusiasts across the River Severn on what was only a century ago the world's longest single-span iron bridge. Note carefully the reflections in the water, best seen when the picture is held in the vertical. On the far bank runs the Worcestershire Way and on the near bank is Eymore Wood, (page 49) near Bewdley.

Part of the huge flight of locks on the Birmingham & Worcester Canal at Tardebigge (see page 144) between Droitwich and Redditch. This remarkable incline incorporates a total of 58 locks which, surprisingly enough, seem to ...

The old Pershore road bridge, near Pershore, as seen from the picnic site beside the A44.

Twisted sycamores, the Four Stones and a solitary cyclist taking a breather - it can only be Adam's Hill, in the Clent Hills (page 28) near Hagley.

Wychbury Hill's own temple of Theseus, just off the busy Hagley–Halesowen A456 road. Designed by James 'Athenian' Stuart, this first Greek revivalist building in Britain was commissioned by Lord Lyttelton of Hagley Hall.

Southstone Rock, Rock Coppice (page 66) near Clifton-upon-Teme almost hidden deep in the Teme Valley is a gigantic, porous, dripping lump of tufa (spongeform rock), packed with hollows and covered in campanulas - sheer magic, and not a little creepy!

Knowles Mill in the Wyre Forest (page 52) near Bewdley is built out of local stone and blends perfectly into the landscape once located down a long winding path through beautiful woodland.

Feckenham Wylde Moor (page 128) just south of Redditch may not be the most picturesque place in Worcestershire but its dense sea of mixed grasses and marsh flowers hides a bed of waterlogged clay which together form one of the richest bird reserves in the county. There is a

The dune system at Hartlebury Common (page 108) near Stourport, showing the unusual, wide expanses of bare red sand. This uncolonised sand-bowl was once a Victorian firing range.

*This ancient pollarded (carefully removed main limbs) oak
has survived for over 500 years and is a firm favourite with
visitors to Worcester and Hereford Countryside Service
Centre at Nunnery Wood (page 97) on the outskirts of
Worcester.*

A contorted chestnut 'old man' of the woods at Piper's Hill (page 123) near Bromsgrove. The Tolkienesque landscape of venerable great trees and dry, open woodland floor is a consequence of wood-pasture (one-time farm animal foraging).

Picking bilberries on - where else - Bilberry Hill in the Lickey Hills range (page 37) near Bromsgrove.

Volunteers at Pepper Wood (page 117), Britain's first community woodland, doing what once came naturally to our ancestors - fully utilising even secondary timber growth, in this case for fenceposts. Visit the wood and buy some!

The towering small-leaved limes at Shrawley Wood (page 110). Relics of warmer climes, these trees which once filled our forests survive at their best here and are regularly coppiced.

Pinnacle Hill

OSL Map 150
GR SO 768/421

OSP SO 64/74
Car parks at Wyche Cutting
GR 769/737 and Wynds
Point GR 763/304

*Access from A449 at Wynds
Point and B4218 Wyche
Cutting.*

*Common Land with superb
views to Herefordshire and
Worcestershire.*

*Excellent ridge top walking
across Malverns.*

*Public Transport: Buses
from Worcester to Malvern.
Trains from Worcester and
Birmingham to Malvern
Link and Barnard's Green.*

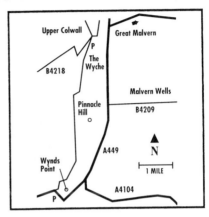

The Wyche Cutting is the ideal
start for an exploration of the hills
south of Worcestershire Beacon.
Here you are over 900 feet above
sea level and the climb to the
highest point of Pinnacle Hill is
gradual and shallow. You can also
reach the top from the southern
end of the ridge at the British
Camp car-park, though the climb
is steeper and the approach less
inviting.

From the Wyche, a flight of steps
leads onto the hillside through a
tunnel of broom and bracken.

Then, without any effort, there
you are on a rocky ridge with
Worcestershire laid out beneath
for your inspection. To the east is
the planned countryside of
Malvern Wells, the neat geometric
fields a product of the commons
enclosures of the 18th century.
The Three Counties showground
is a prominent feature especially
when dotted with marquees. To
the south is an avenue of trees
marking the course of the old railway from Malvern to Upton,
opened in 1864 and closed in
1952. Where it cuts into the
fields, it has left a series of trian-
gular segments of pasture hung
like bunting along its length.

The current railway lies beneath
you in a 1500 foot tunnel.
Opened in 1926, it shadows the
original tunnel, now overgrown
and colonised by bats. The narrow bore passes through hard

granite known as syenite as well as layers of marl and limestone and was cut by hammer and steam drill. It was begun in 1857 and completed four years later; the full story of its construction is described in a fact sheet available from the Tourist Information Centre.

Malvern's name is derived from "moel bryn", meaning bare hill, an apt description of the ridgetop. Vegetation will grow, but has to contend with thousands of hikers each month; in the more exposed spots it abandons the effort. Nevertheless, there are plants to be found. Sand spurrey is a particularly pleasing flower of the most eroded pathsides, although its tiny pink blooms go unnoticed by most visitors. So too do the grey lichens which encrust the jagged outcrops. The commonest of these is crottle which yields a yellow dye when mixed with human urine - who first discovered this is not on record!

For the most part the hillsides are dominated by stands of gorse, bracken and willowherb none of which can be penetrated easily. Only where the soft cushions of wavy hair grass, the commonest grass on the Malverns,grow can you wander off the beaten track. In summer, the grass provides such a dense cover that the hills are tinged dusky pink, turning to pale straw in autumn.

As you head southwards, the path dips past Thirds Land, the only conifer plantation on the hills. Redpolls and siskins feed in the winter larches while ravens have been seen overhead. Even if you cannot see these huge crows, their hollow grunts ring around the slopes. To the west are the woods and small fields of Herefordshire. Modern maps do not record the fact that you are walking along the old county boundary, the course of the "Red Earl's Dyke". In places you can still see the remains of the ramparts, built in 1287 by Gilbert de Clare, 7th Earl of Gloucester. His defensive action began with a dispute between the earl and the Bishop of Hereford who claimed hunting rights over land along the west side of the hill. Eventually, the argument was settled in law in favour of the bishop. The "Red Earl" was so incensed by the decision that he constructed a steep boundary ditch to prevent game escaping onto the bishop's land, even arming it with sharp palings to guarantee passage onto his land only.

From the summit of Pinnacle Hill, the ground slopes gently towards Wynds Point and the Beacon Hotel. Maybe it was from here that Piers the Ploughman had his vision of "a fair field full of folk". William Langland's 14th century allegory remains a classic of English literature, an examination of the conflicts of social order, religion and wealth.

The stroll to Wynds Point is pleasant but unexceptional, illuminated by the Iron-Age hill fort on Herefordshire Beacon, stepped like a ziggurat and swarming with people at weekends.

For a different return route, you can take the lower paths along the Malvern side of the hill. These wind pleasantly among the gorse above Holy Well, before regaining the ridge at Thirds Land.

Chase End and Ragged Stone Hill

OSL Map 150
GR SO 760/359

OSP SO 63/73

On minor road south of A438 at Hollybush.

Private: Wooded hillside at the southern extremity of the Malverns. Superb views and woodland walk.

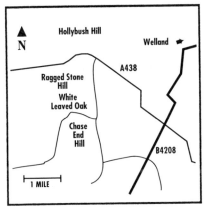

On busy summer days, the larger Malverns are anything but quiet, so lovers of solitude head southwards to the tail-end of the spine. Here on Chase End Hill, the counties of Gloucestershire, Herefordshire and Worcestershire meet on as remote a hilltop as you could wish for, a mini-Malvern to explore at your leisure.

The easiest way to reach this remote spot by car is from the A438 west of Eastnor. At Hollybush take the minor road south for a mile and then the first road west to a cluster of cottages at Whiteleaved Oak. Park carefully here and walk alongside Cider Mill cottage on the path indicated by the Gloucestershire County Council sign - this is foreign territory!

A dark and tempting path between high hedges and flanked by nettle-leaved bellflowers soon opens out onto a bracken-clad hillside. Ahead the ground rises steeply to the triangulation point at the modest summit, only 600 feet above sea-level. Erosion is a problem in spite of Chase End's remoteness, witness the tongue-shaped grooves gouged from the turf.

On top, you regain Worcestershire, though the surrounding countryside is Gloucester and Hereford. Away to the west are the Black Mountains, to the east the Cotswold Hills. Flat farmland has replaced the marshland which was once an extension of the Severn estuary. As if borne by nostalgia, gulls still commute upriver along the chain of the hills, riding the air currents. These birds are

77

supposed to appear inland when the coastal weather is rough, but in fact are regular winter visitors and scavenge on household waste at tips. Several pairs of lesser black-backed gulls now nest on rooftops in the centre of Worcester.

Rabbits are everywhere, resistant to myxomatosis and breeding like, well, rabbits. Together with sheep and people they have eliminated grass on the bare crown of the hill so that all you will find is a thin coating of lichen and sorrel, liberally fertilised with rabbit-droppings.

One building demands attention. Shrouded in trees to the west are the crenelated towers of Eastnor Castle, a Georgian copy completed in 1817 and designed by Samuel Smirke, the architect of the British Museum. Its imposing grey battlements are reflected in the waters of an impressive lake and red deer graze its parkland. The castle is open to the public throughout summer.

A broad lawn leads south from the top to join the minor road to Bromsberrow. You can return to your start by turning right along this lane or by taking the woodland path to the left through plantations of spruce, chestnut and hornbeam. The round trip is about two miles in length and offers gentle walking all the way.

The woodland path emerges on the lane a few hundred yards east of your starting point. Walk uphill and turn right on the left-hand bend and you can climb the wooded slopes of Raggedstone Hill. Oaks soon give way to the bare and curiously forked hilltop. Raggedstone is notorious for one thing - its shadow brings death on whomever it falls. The hill is said to be haunted by the shade of a monk from Little Malvern Priory who committed the ultimate sin of falling in love. As a punishment, he was condemned to crawl daily to the summit of the hill, until one day he could take no more and cursed Raggedstone and those on whom its shadow should fall. Now even this shadow is reputed to assume a cowled monkish shape and is there a certain symbolism in the bare crown of the summit, surrounded by a tonsure of oaks?

Castlemorton Common

OSL Map 150
GR SO 770/380

OSP SO 63/73

Along B4208 south of Welland village.

Largely grassy common - ideal for picnics and kites. Access to Gullet quarry and Swinyard Hill. Good fine walking, gentle gradients on Berrow Down at western end.

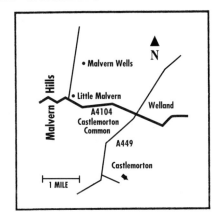

Everyone knows the Malvern Hills, stark and unmissable as they rise from the Severn plain. Rather fewer people take time to visit the Malvern commons, though they can plainly be seen from the southern hilltops, patched with russet bracken and dotted with settlements. Some have been enveloped by the towns of Malvern Link and Malvern Wells, but others, such as Castlemorton, remain wild and unenclosed, survivors of a medieval landscape.

Castlemorton lies on the fringes of Welland village. Head south on the B4208 and, where the fences give out, the common begins. Wandering sheep are a hazard for drivers, (if only geneticists could breed a sheep with road-sense!) and are owned by the many farmers who have the right to graze livestock on the common. As the many notices warn you, dogs must be kept on leads or they may be destroyed.

The best point from which to explore the area is from the minor road leading right from the main road as you travel south from Welland. If you park on the higher parts of Berrow Down, you are ideally placed for climbing Swinyard Hill or investigating the recesses of the Gullet quarry. Be warned that if you own a Volkswagen minibus or similar vehicle, you may be watched closely by local residents. In summer 1992 Castlemorton achieved national coverage when 20,000 people variously described as hippies, ravers and New Age travellers occupied the common for a few days.

Down by the main road are the roughest spots, watered by

streams and rich in wildlife. This is no sandy waste strewn with heather, but a clayey grassland with a huge variety of flowers. Some, like the corky-fruited water dropwort, a white parsley, are rare and relatively inconspicuous. Others, like the black poplar trees are much more obvious but almost as rare. Over eighty of these trees dot the common, most pollarded into knobbled green domes, like enormous leafy lollipops. They represent the largest concentration of the species in Britain.

Because black poplars need both sexes to achieve pollination, they are easy to eradicate accidentally. On Castlemorton they huddle to-gether for protection, hunched conspiratorially around ponds, but need have no fear - the Conservators still pollard them for use in the neighbouring villages.

Follow the minor road across the common and you eventually reach a dead-end at the Gullet. Here is a disused quarry, very busy in summer when swimmers launch themselves recklessly into the pool below. The Pre-Cambrian rock is laid bare exposing outcrops of schist, veins of pink felspar and white strata of quartz. Unfortunately, you cannot reach the hilltop from this angle. Instead follow the open bracken-lined route from the slopes of the Common to climb Swinyard Hill.

Hollybed Common

OSL Map 150
GR SO 775/370

OSP SO 63/73

On no-through road off B4208 half a mile north of Birts Street.

Large open common with mill-pond and excellent views to Malvern Hills. Good flat walking with link to Castlemorton Common.

Public Transport: Bus from Great Malvern.

Almost continuous with Castlemorton, this is a wide, flat expanse of grass and gorse, perfect for exploring, but rarely visited except by commons connoisseurs. This is a pity, for Hollybed Common or Golden Valley as it is known locally, is an historic landscape reminiscent of pre-enclosure Worcestershire.

You can reach it by travelling south of Castlemorton Common on the B4208 and by taking the no-through road signposted to your right after about one mile. Cottages and small dwellings line the road which soon peters out into a gravelled track. You can park on the verge here after surrendering the small charge requested by the Conservators. The first and most attractive feature is the pool, stocked with fish and understandably popular with anglers. Coot, mallard and even grey herons are here regularly and allow a close approach.

To the north is the common itself, dry and unyielding with little to offer of agricultural value. For this reason it would have been low on the list when much of Worcestershire was enclosed in the late 18th century by Act of Parliament. Many of the smallholdings had their origins as squatter settlements in the 18th and 19th centuries. Now grazed by black-faced sheep and a multitude of rabbits, the common is a mosaic of grass and scrub.

Why Golden Valley? Go in late summer when the western gorse is in bloom and you will see acres of golden-yellow blooms, infused with the soft taint of coconut in hot weather.

Footpaths cross the grassland but are indistinct and you are free to wander at will. With the backing hills as landmarks, you can reach Castlemorton Common by heading north-west, but as you go, take time to examine the local wildlife. It's a curious terrain, bumpy with anthills and shorn to the bone by livestock, but nevertheless, manages to support a flourishing natural history. Harebells, lady's bedstraw and wild thyme grow on the anthills in fragrant "midsummer cushions". Green woodpeckers seem to be everywhere and bound off yelping as you flush them. In spring and autumn, wheatears flash white rumps over the turf. These pert passerines have nothing to do with wheat - their name is derived from the old English "white-arse".

Meadow pipits, linnets and yellowhammers are all regular breeders in the archipelagoes of gorse, though many leave this unproductive heathscape in winter to forage on arable land.

At any time of year the valley is good walking country, offering wide open space and solitude.

Ravenshill Wood

OSL Map 150
GR SO 740/539

OSP SO 65/75

Along minor road south from between A44 Knightsford Bridge and Alfrick.

Private. Oak and conifer woodland on limestone hill. Two trails, often steep and occasionally muddy in winter. Visitor centre open March to October.

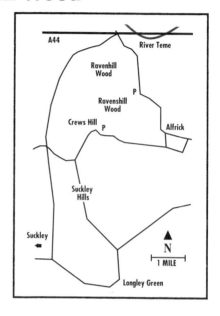

Privately owned nature reserves are rare enough in Worcestershire- those which welcome the public are even rarer. Ravenshill Wood, near Alfrick is not only set in the county's oldest landscape, but allows you to explore a magnificent tract of ancient woodland, thanks to the co-operation of its owners.

The reserve, which lies on the limestone Suckley Hills, was created by the late Elizabeth Barling, a keen naturalist and active member of the Worcestershire Nature Conservation Trust.Its modern management is now carried out by wardens Colin and Sue Clark who maintain the wildlife interest and encourage visitors.

That you are welcome at Ravenshill is never in doubt. Go between Easter and October and the visitor centre will be open, crammed with all you need for a walk in the woods. Here are free trail maps, parking for up to 15 cars and picnic tables. There's also a blackboard updated regularly to feature the latest sightings and, if you have trouble hunting down helleborines or watching for warblers, consult the extensive library of natural history books. Paths through the wood are of glutinous clay and can be frustratingly slippery in wet weather, so the wardens have provided a range of wellies for you to borrow. Not everyone will be amused by the collection of stuffed animals which stare glassy-eyed as you approach the donations box, but they have all met natural ends and are indisputably popular with children.

Two trails have been designed to provide either a gentle stroll or a more energetic uphill walk. Both lead from the picnic area and are clearly marked by signposts. The red trail is a half-mile long and the blue trail, leading off it, a mile longer.

A few steps into the wood will tell you that Ravenshill has not escaped the relentless tide of coniferisation. Thankfully, the native trees are re-asserting themselves, but there are stands of norway spruce and western hemlock remaining. Some of the tallest trees are the poplars at the start of the red trail. Planted over many areas of the county in damp valleys, they were used for matchmaking before the disappearance of England's Glory and Bryant & May. Naked ladies await you at this point, but don't expect too sensational a sight- this is the name given to the leafless pink blooms of meadow saffron, a scarce autumn-flowering crocus. Look for it in September or in spring when its sheaves of shiny leaves bunch along the rides.

Nearby is a specially-constructed pond where smooth and palmate newts float in spring. Woodland flowers are especially showy at this season when dog violets, celandines and wood anemones

line the paths. Great pendulous sedge is everywhere, as grand as it sounds lending an almost tropical ambience to the woodscape- you almost reach for your machete!

For a spell of botanical oneupmanship, try learning to distinguish between barren and wild strawberries. The first bears downy leaves, petals shorter than the sepals beneath them, and a sense of disappointment, for, as its name suggests, it has no berries. Real wild strawberries have shiny leaves, larger flowers, often in clusters and delicious fruits, though there are never enough of them. The path winds upwards, well marked by blue trail signs and you may at times be grateful for a seat. There are none however, until you reach the viewpoint at the topmost corner of the wood. To the south are the soft hummocks of Old Storridge Common crowned with oakwoods and beyond, looming magisterially, the three northernmost peaks of the Malverns.

From here it's all downhill, through groves of sessile oak, where in early summer you may catch a glimpse of the delicate wood white butterfly, a Ravenshill speciality. The complete walk takes little more than an hour at a gentle stroll. Before you leave don't forget to record any interesting sightings in the visitors' book.

Suckley Hills

OSL Map 150
GR SO 734/532

OSP SO 65/75

On minor roads west of Alfrick.

Wooded limestone ridges rich in wild flowers. Paths steep and often muddy at any time of year.

To experience the true feel of the Worcestershire "wildwood", the ancient forests which have all but disappeared since the New Stone Age, you can do no better than visit the Suckley Hills. Nowhere in the county is the rural tapestry so varied.Here on the ridges of Silurian limestone which formed the beds of coral seas 400 million years ago , survive the last vestiges of truly ancient woodland. Even here you need to pick your route with care. Many dark deeds have been committed in the name of commercial forestry and few woods have escaped the taint of coniferisation.

The approach, through the lanes of Alfrick and Longley Green takes you through a patchwork of old hopyards, arable, pasture and small woods, a truly eclectic mixture of countryside. The hops have declined because of the ravages of Verticillium "wilt" and all hop fields are strictly out of

bounds to walkers, who may introduce the fungal spores on their clothes or feet.

The hills are all privately owned, but are threaded with a variety of footpaths, one of which is the Worcestershire Way. They are best divided into two sections, one offering flattish walking, the other a steep circular route with the bonus of an excellent pub en route.

The short and fairly level walk is through Ravenhill Wood, confusingly close to Ravenshill Wood, described in the previous account. Your best starting point is from Crews Hill, a mile west of Alfrick. Parking is restricted along the narrow lane crossing the ridge, so take care to avoid blocking driveways. At the highest point of the lane, take the bridleway leading north. The path is bordered with attractive cottages while to the left is an apple orchard. Disused diggings line the path, small-scale extraction of limestone for domestic use or for lime-kilns.

At the first of these pits, turn right past a bungalow to enter the dark domain of Ravenhill Wood.

There is probably no better stand in the county of Worcestershire's rarest tree than along the sloping track through this wood. In May, the massive trunks and branches of coppiced large-leaved lime tower overhead in graceful arches, bearing sheaves of downy leaves, soft to the touch. Large-leaved lime is native to a scatter of British counties in undisturbed woods to the west and north. Like its small-leaved cousin it is an indicator of ancient woodland and grows on steep uncultivable slopes. Once it was more frequent, but now is out of step with our climate finding it difficult to germinate from seed. In the Suckley area it is fairly well-distributed, even occurring as a hedgerow tree, which indicates that the hedges in question were assarted, that is carved from blocks of existing woodland. Some of these venerable limes have twenty coppiced stems and may be two hundred years old. Here in their last domain, they are a far cry from the hybrid limes which border suburban avenues, raining a sticky aphid honeydew onto cars and passers-by. One last word about limes - their leaves can be eaten in sandwiches, though young ones tend to tickle the palate.

The path descends gently to join a track surfaced with shale. You can follow this along the footpath downhill to emerge on the lane next to Ravenshill Nature Reserve, but be prepared for a two-mile walk along the lane back to Crews Hill. For a shorter and gentler walk which keeps your altitude, bear left keeping an orchard and fields to your right until the woods give out and you rejoin the Worcestershire Way. Another left turn will take you back to Crews Hill.

For a taste of ancient woodland at its most varied and a steeper walk, follow the Worcestershire Way south along the Suckley ridge. A few steps into the trees reveal the extraordinary variety of the flowers. Spring is the time to visit when the woodland floor is carpeted with bluebells, stitchwort, celandines wild violets and a beautiful dead-nettle called yellow archangel. Wood spurge and sanicle also flourish here beneath both species of lime and wild service trees. Yews are scattered throughout the wood; these iron-timbered conifers were usually kept by foresters to store their timber beneath, thus keeping it dry. Conifers soon take over, mingled improbably with the natives and there is even a plantation of copper beech, surely one of our most unappealing trees with its crown of blackish summer foliage.

The going can be sticky underfoot on the limy ridge, so watch your pace. Soon the path turns left, crosses the lane and climbs into Hallhouse Coppice. Follow the Worcestershire Way markers for just over a mile and you come to Longley Green, after descending a steep bank deep within the wood - travel the other way on a wet winter day and it seems endless. After a refreshing stopover at the Nelson Inn, you can retrace your steps or follow the lanes through Suckley.

The Knapp and Papermill

OSL Map 150
GR SO 749/522

OSP SO 65/75

Along minor road from west of A4103 at Bransford.

WNCT. Meadows, streamside and woodland walks in the Leigh Brook valley. Excellent for wildlife and solitude. Information at Knapp Cottage.

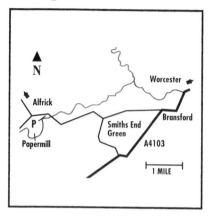

Although it sounds like two places, this is a single magnificent nature reserve owned and managed by the WNCT. A fascinating mix of habitats includes hay meadows, lush valley woods, a trout stream and an old orchard. Even without the wildlife it would be idyllic, a nostalgic reminder of old Worcestershire.

Sunk deep in a valley between Alfrick Pound and Old Storridge Common, this is a place to relish, with low-level walking and sunny picnic spots. Best of all, few people have discovered it - go in the week and you will most likely be the only visitors.

Approach lanes are all narrow and parking is limited, so take care to use the lay-by where the Leigh Brook crosses the Bransford to Alfrick road. Across the road is the WNCT entrance sign

and map of the reserve. As you enter you could be forgiven for thinking you are trespassing in a private cottage garden. Tangles of mallow, Aaron's rod and anchusa lead to The Knapp Cottage itself. The front porch doubles miraculously as an information centre and is crammed with facts about the reserve, from geological curiosities to recent records. Best of all there are cans of cold drink, essential on a sweltering summer's day. A trail guide written by the WNCT is an invaluable companion.

Past the cottage the garden ends abruptly. Through a gate is an old orchard of Annie Elizabeth cooking apples. Winter sees the arrival of Scandinavian fieldfares and redwings, squabbling noisily over the windfalls. Grey-lichened boughs shade a springtime carpet of violets, primroses and cowslips.

This last plant's name is a corruption of "cowslop" because it chooses well-fertilised places in which to grow. Cattle are often loose in the orchard to control scrub, so be careful where you step!

To the left an inconspicuous path leads to the county's only Kingfisher hide. A wooden observation hut has been built opposite a steep bank in which the birds usually nest and a few silent minutes will give sightings of this avian jewel. Escaped mink also prowl the brook margins, preying on voles and young birds. Although the Leigh Brook runs clear and deep, all is not well. Pollution from agricultural fertilisers and other sources has seeped into the stream's catchment area, causing blooms of brown algae. This coats the pebbles and uses oxygen, reducing supplies for fish and insects. Dippers have already gone, but kingfishers survive on the remaining brown trout. These fish have been seen climbing the weir, built over 200 years ago to power a mill.

Beyond the weir is Daffodil Meadow, a damp pasture planted with cultivated bulbs by a previous owner. Although showy, they pale into insignificance next to one of Worcestershire's rarest plants. Spires of night-blue monkshood lurk beneath the willows and alders, more delicate than garden varieties but equally as deadly. Gerard, the 16th Century herbalist was unusually blunt about its qualities of this plant - "if you eat monkshood it kills you"

Fringing woods encircle the large hay meadow ahead. Big Meadow was once called Great Epiphany because its rent was due on 6th January, Epiphany Day. Arched across the brook nearby is Pivany Bridge. The meadow cries out to be picnicked in, but the wardens prefer you to wait until haymaking has finished. In Summer the field is a rich patchwork of purple knapweed, yellow bird's foot trefoil and ox-eye daisies, reminders of the old hay meadows which have been reduced by 95% in Britain. Modern farming methods cannot balance floral diversity with yield requirements and so most old meadows have been replaced with monocultures of rye grass. Living museums such as Papermill seem to be the only house-room we can afford to spare these precious habitats and their wildlife.

Ancient woods beckon west of the field, full of wych elm, wild service and small-leaved lime. Even better is large-leaved lime, distinguished by its hairy spring leaves. Defying gravity on the steep slopes are massive cherries their tiger-striped bark shining on sunny winter days. Leigh Brook chuckles over its stony bed, and in sunlit spots, navy demoiselle damselflies vie for resting places.

After a few minutes you reach Papermill Meadow, the focal point of which is Papermill Cottage. It is uninhabited, but has been rebuilt in part by wardens and volunteers. Once known as Gunwick Mill, it was part of a larger complex washed away by a great twenty-foot flood in 1852. In the garden are the remains of a cider press and nearby a group of old pear trees. Their fruit is tough and indigestible, but yields pear-cider or perry.

At this turning point, you can retrace your steps or complete the trail by heading for the north-west corner of the meadow. Tor Coppice is an oakwood, cut on a twenty year cycle to favour woodland plants. A path returns to the orchard parallel to the north edge of Big Meadow, along the wood borders. Look out for spotted flycatchers here, sallying out from trees to chase insects which they catch with an audible "snap".

Soon you are back at the Knapp Cottage; don't forget to record your sightings in the diary!

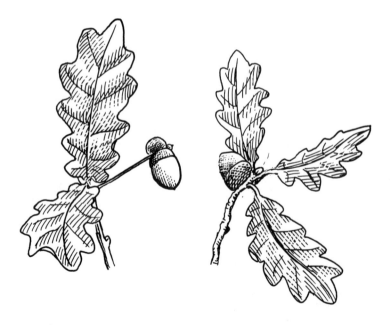

Pedunculate Oak (left) and Sessile Oak

Old Hills Common

OSL Map 150
GR SO 829/487

OSP SO 84/94

Along B4224 from Powick to Upton-on-Severn.

MHDC. Scrub, open grassland and woodland with excellent views across Severn Valley and to Malvern Hills. Good for picnics and walking. Paths sloping but good at all seasons.

Public Transport: MRW bus from Worcester to Powick.

Most travellers flash through this pleasant common en route from Worcester to Upton-on-Severn. It is easy to miss, a relatively small unfenced piece of scrub, immediately south of Callow End on the B4424. Most of its visitors are local, walking the dog or strolling around the common's neatly mown footpaths. The care of its grassland and woods is undertaken by the Malvern Hills Conservators, who ask in return, a modest parking charge.

You can walk the entire perimeter on both sides of the road in a brisk and breathless hour, but the main "selling-point" of Old Hills is its anonymity. To the east is a quiet expanse of hawthorn and bracken where you can picnic at

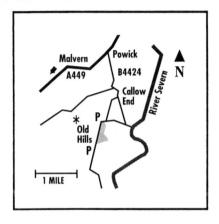

your leisure, undisturbed by anything, save perhaps for the traffic on the road beneath. Old common rights have declined; you may see a few horses or a gaggle of grazing geese but the thick tangle of scrub bears witness to a common in decline. Now the Conservators are the saviour of this and many other commons, retaining their ancient character for all to enjoy. Amongst the scrub are a number of craggy oaks, some dead for years and shattered by frost and fungus. Jackdaws nest in the crannies of their greying boughs and magpies machine-gun walkers with a vocal volley of abuse. As in most parts of the county, magpies have increased dramatically in recent years. Public opinion, fuelled by local press and landowners, has accused these birds of heinous crimes, usually involving the slaughter of nestling songbirds.

The ill-founded persecution continues despite a detailed survey by the British Trust for Ornithology which has proved that magpies have little or no effect on songbird numbers overall. Much more damage is done by cats, often owned by those who blame the magpie! You may, though not at Old hills, see a live magpie fluttering in a cage known as a Larsen trap, designed to lure other magpies to their destruction. Amazingly, there is no law against this activity, though landowners are obliged to provide water and food for lure birds.

Certainly, magpies have not discouraged the birds here. Blackcaps and garden warblers are common and the grey, bandit-masked lesser whitethroat skulks in fringing hedgerows.Butterflies are frequent too; in May look out for the tiny green hairstreak, our only species with green pigment.

The view from the eastern fringe takes in Kempsey Common, ablaze with gorse in spring, and the M5 motorway. To the west of the road you can see the Malvern Hills and the decommissioned Powick Hospital, with its red-brick tower.

Marsh Common and Dunstall Common

OSL Map 150 GR Marsh
Common SO 892/421

OSP SO 84/94 GR Dunstall
Common SO 885/429

Off Marsh Common off
A4104 east of M5 at
Baughton Hill. Dunstall
Common along minor road,
east of M4 from A38 (T) at
Earl's Groome.

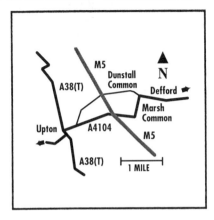

Private: Small roadside
common linked by a bridle-
way. Short walk of about
one hour via woodland at
Brierley Hill.

These two small commons are
treated here as one because they
are practically neighbours and
neither has quite enough to offer.
Taken together they provide a
pleasant short walk of about two
miles.

You will find them just east of the
M5 motorway. Marsh Common is
the most accessible, alongside the
A4104 at Baughton Hill. It isn't
much to look at, a damp and
overgrown field backed by an indifferent mixed woodland, but
there are a few wildlife gems.
Parking is tricky to say the least
and you would be safer to continue along the A4104 eastwards
to the next left turn. Soon you are
on Dunstall Common, though you
may see a mere widening of the

verge and pass it by. That is all
there is and it would be tempting
to drive on were it not for the impressive sham castle by the laneside. Three towers of ivy-clad
beige stone set in the middle of
nowhere do demand attention,
especially when there is no at-
tached building. The castle is a
folly, built in the late 18th century
by the Earl of Coventry who
owned the nearby Croome Estate.
It's an attractive construction with
elegant trefoil windows and turns
an otherwise drab roadside common into a place of interest.

Having inspected it, you can return to Marsh Common along the
bridleway leading past Red Deer
Farm. This crosses a pasture and
enters the mixed woodland of
Brierley Hill. Be prepared for a
struggle-even the passage of
horses has not tamed the vegetation and you will be grabbed as

91

you proceed by a hundred hooks and burrs. Woolly jumpers will need to be combed out carefully afterwards! The track is muddy at all times, though there is compensation in the form of peacock and brimstone butterflies which feast on the burdock flowers.

The bridleway disgorges you onto the A4104 at Baughton Hill from where it is a short walk to Marsh Common. Picnics are generally out of the question on this private common, mainly because the grass grows fast and luxuriantly and is too high to penetrate. At the far end of the common is a bridleway which skirts a wood and emerges on the lane east of Dunstall Common. Two minute's walking will return you to your start.

Wood Mouse

Normoor Common

OSL Map 150
GR SO 862/472

OSP SO 84/94

Along minor road east of A38(T) at Kempsey.

Private small grassy common adjacent to motorway. Best visited in conjunction with Kerswell Green and Ashmoor Common.

Public transport. MRW buses from Worcester to Kempsey.

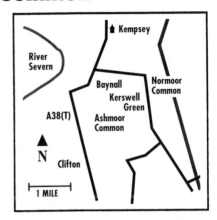

The village of Kempsey, a few miles south of Worcester on the A38, borders a clutch of commons, mostly to the east of the M5. Normoor lies to the west, cruelly separated from its neighbours by the motorway. To reach it, turn second left on leaving the village to the south. This lane cuts through the common after passing a magnificent brick-built country house at the Nash.

West of the lane is an open field, dotted with purple knapweed and golden hay rattle, alive with bobbing meadow brown butterflies in summer. Mowing keeps the char-

acter of this patch, but the opposite side of the road tells a different story. Here the common's nature has been compromised by inappropriate planting. There really is no excuse for the aliens such as whitebeam, grey alder and false acacia which have been imposed on the verge. Look beyond these and you will see the invading elms, oaks and brambles colonising from the fringing hedges: amazing as it may seem to many landowners, our native trees are capable of propagating themselves!

Parking sites are few, but there is a little more room at Kerswell Green, a few hundred yards to the south.

93

Ashmoor Common

OSL Map 150
GR SO 854/465

OSP SO 84/94

Along public footpath from Keswell Green, a quarter of a mile south of Normoor Common.

Private. Secluded Common with spring. Access limited, but rich in wildlife and good for walks to Clifton and Severn Stroke. Path difficult to find over wet ground - a challenge!

Public Transport MRW buses from Worcester to Upton-on-Severn.

This common is simply a delight, hidden by farmland and rarely visited. It is crossed by one public footpath so that access is limited, but may be included in a circular walk taking in Kerswell Green and Normoor Common.

Beautiful thatched cottages border Kerswell Green, a tiny settlement south of Kempsey. On the map it looks perilously close to the M5, but is remarkably peaceful. Although small, this hamlet can boast among its past families the Winslows. In 1620, Edward Winslow and his brother Gilbert set sail aboard the Mayflower with the Pilgrim Fathers. Edward played a key role in establishing one of the first British colonies in North America of which he became governor.

The neatly mown green is picturesque, but unwelcoming- where are the public footpath signs?. An O/S map is more than useful here - it's vital if you want to reach Ashmoor Common. To get there take the gravelled drive just north of the telephone kiosk.

It leads along a private drive past a thatched and timber-framed house and from there through a cornfield. After a few yards it leaves the track to plunge downhill through the corn. Ahead over a bryony-clad stile is the damp luxuriance of Ashmoor. The contrast with the surrounding arable is immediately obvious. Behind are the dry deserts of barley, ahead spring-fed fields of thistle and bramble, starred with flowers and bordered by willows. In mid-summer,by far the best season, the thistle patches are alive with butterflies and bees. Little owls glare fiercely from the pollards against a backcloth of the Malvern Hills, blue in the haze. Away to the north the common stretches toward the Kempsey road. It may be rich in wildlife, but this is a neglected common now grazed by a few horses and receiving little attention. Where short cropped turf once grew, there are now hummocks of thorny bramble and rank hedges. Whitethroats and linnets find perfect nest-sites and, if you are lucky and under forty-five, you may hear the thin reeling of a grasshopper warbler. The high-pitched continuous song sounds like a fishing-line winding in and becomes inaudible the older you get.

From here, you can return by your outward route or continue through the common to Clifton village. Turn south and then east on the first public footpath and you will reach Birch Green. At Naunton Farm, any northbound footpath will bring back to Kerswell Green and your starting point.

A ring around Worcester

A radius of about ten miles around Worcester City includes a wide variety of sites in the heart of the county. These range from ancient lowland woods such as Monkwood and Trench to sandy heaths such as Hartlebury Common and even two superb woodlands in the city itself. The accessibility of the area makes it an ideal place in which to begin your exploration of the Worcestershire countryside.

Worcester Woods Country Park
Nunnery Wood
Perry Wood

Powick Hams

Stonehall and Kempsey Commons

Monkwood
Monkwood Green

Hartlebury Common

Shrawley Wood

Chaddesley Wood
Purshull Green

Pepper Wood

Trench Wood

Piper's Hill

Worcester Woods Country Park

Within Worcester city limits and partly engulfed by houses, this is unusual countryside indeed. The Country Park is managed by HWCS and comprises two woods, an events field and three old hay meadows on the eastern fringe of the city. Careful planning has resulted in a mix of attractions which make a day spent here enjoyable for all the family and if that sounds hackneyed, try it! The woods are very different in appeal and ease of access, and since they are as yet unconnected by a waymarked route, are treated separately here.

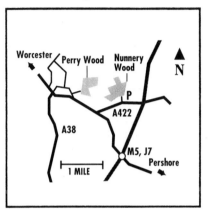

Nunnery Wood

OSL Map 150
GR SO 877/543

OSP SO 85/95

Off A422, off Stratford Road, half a mile East of Worcester. Signposted at entrance to County Hall.

HWCC. Ancient semi-natural woodland with excellent paths. Wheelchair trail. Visitor centre with information, toilets and refreshments. Events field and children's adventure playground. Map and leaflet from HWCC

The entrance to Nunnery Wood and the Countryside Centre has to be the most unlikely of any described in this book. Tucked discreetly behind the glass and masonry of County Hall, the wood itself cannot be seen from the old A422 and you need to follow the brown tourist signs to the Countryside Centre to reach it. New road layouts have made this area unrecognisable from the O/S map, so follow the County Hall signs once in the vicinity.

Before you explore the 50-acre wood, a visit to the Countryside Centre is a must. It's full of information about the Country Park, is

97

the base for the park's ranger service and has an admirable cafe. The adjacent events field and surrounding mounds are ideal for kite-flying or picnicking, and children will soon exhaust themselves on the ingeniously designed play area. If you like planning your days out, ask for details of the wide programme of events which include green fairs, guided walks and even car-boot sales.

Free maps of the woods are available, including a leaflet for wheelchair users which illustrates the attractions of the easy access trail. From the minute you enter Nunnery Wood, its age impresses. These oaks may not be large - nearly all were felled in the 1940s - but they are unquestionably survivors. Most trunks arise from a mossy stool, a sign of past coppicing, which ensured the survival of this ancient wood. Hazel is the classic coppice shrub, growing throughout, so that visibility is confined to just a few yards into the green depths and forget that County hall or the city is anywhere near.

Now coppicing has been reintroduced to benefit wildlife and you will see scrubby areas and clearings enlivening the denser places. There is one very old tree on the eastern edge, a splendid gnarled oak, probably pollarded 500 years ago and still going strong. Other indicators of ancient woodland include wild service trees, relatives of the rowan with maple-shaped leaves. The berries are brown and acerbic and were once bletted - ripened until they rotted -

and used as ingredients in beer. Some say that the name service derives from the Latin for beer "cerevisia", others that it is a corruption of the scientific name Sorbus. An old name for the tree was "chequers" because the bark splits into tessellations and was the origin of pubs of that name. Nearly all the service trees are on the woodland edge which may indicate that the wood has once been ploughed. Certainly its centre has a washboard texture reminiscent of "ridge and furrow".

As you follow the woodland paths, you will come across curious wooden poles decorated with numbers and iron bars. These are ingredients in a unique orienteering system devised by Edgar Powell, ask at the Centre for details of this fascinating pastime. You will also see a surprising amount of wildlife from squirrels and foxes to chiffchaffs and woodpeckers. A small pool, dug for clay, is now home to a population of great crested newts, protected by law.

At the western edge, there are playing fields and beyond a drab council estate behind which you can just see the trees of Perry Wood, the other part of the country park. There are footpaths through the houses, but you will need a map to find your way.

If you grow tired of the trees, make your way back to the centre and explore Hornhill Meadows. These old hay fields are rich in flowers and, in spite of the new eastern by-pass, make an excellent picnic spot.

Perry Wood

OSL Map 150
GR SO 864/544
OSP SO 85/95

Along Perry Wood Walk, off Wylds Lane, Worcester - one mile east of city centre.

WCC. Ancient bluebell rich woodland and adjacent grassland within Worcester. Good views of the city - picnic areas. Paths steep on Western edge, but generally good. Map and leaflet from HWCC.

There's nothing rural about Perry Wood. Squeezed between a housing estate and a factory, it has been absorbed into Worcester and is now owned by the City Council. However, in spite of its isolated location, it is ancient woodland - there is even a documentary reference for 969 A.D. The wood is named after its pear-trees, some of which still grow there and for the drink which was obtained from the fruit. At the battle of Agincourt, the banner of the Worcestershire soldiers sported a pear-tree in fruit, so the drink may have been fermented then. Certainly, when Queen Elizabeth visited the Worcester in 1575, a pear-tree in fruit was placed in the city centre for decoration. The queen took this as a sign of a law-abiding citizenry to leave such a tempting sight untampered with, and henceforth the pear was incorporated into the Worcester arms.

Back to the wood. Perry is on a steep north-facing scarp, one reason for its survival. If you stroll through from Perry Wood Walk in spring you cannot fail to be impressed by the sheets of bluebells and the luxuriance of the wild service trees. There is even small-leaved lime, that classic indicator of ancient woods. Although the wood is managed officially by HWCS, it is unofficially cut by adjoining residents often to the detriment of the trees. There is, though, some historic justice in this haphazard coppicing - their ancestors may have carried out the self-same practice, albeit to better effect.

It won't take long to complete the short circuit of the wood or admire the view across the city below. However, if you linger late on a dank autumn evening, and are receptive to such things, you may sense the presence of a Roundhead's shade in the gloom. Perry Wood was used as a battery by Cromwell before the Battle of Worcester in 1651 and fragments of military armour and even cannonballs have been found here. Charles was routed , and fled the "Faithful City" to become a fugitive for nine years. The full story of this decisive battle and its eventual outcome is told at the nearby Commandery - don't miss it!

Powick Hams

OSL 150 GR SO 835/523

OSP SO 85/95

*Off A449 South of Lower
Wick, Worcester*

*Private/Section 9 Common.
Over 400 acres of pasture
and riverside walking. Good
paths with seats and steps
looking across to Worces-
ter.*

*Public Transport: MRW
buses 23 24 44 45 46 223*

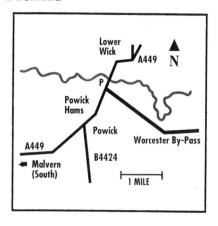

When we envisage common land,
we tend to associate it with
scrubby, often unkempt grassland
or heath. Usually it overlies poor
and unproductive soil and is left
ungrazed. If this is your interpretation, Powick Hams will be a
great surprise.

As you leave Worcester on the
A449 Malvern road, you cross
the bridge over the River Teme.
To the east is the new south
Worcester by-pass, a causeway
over the Severn flood-plain. To
the west are a group of lush
meadows divided by pollard willows - these are Powick Hams.

To reach them, you need to walk
along the disused road which
crosses the old Powick bridge,
built in the 15th century. A public
footpath leads from here along

the southern bank of the Teme
through sheep-filled fields; the notice on the entrance gate warns
you to keep dogs on leads and is
signed "steward of the manor"

Why, then, are these obviously
fertile pastures common land?
The explanation is probably that
they were once Lammas meadows. We use the term meadow
rather loosely nowadays to refer
to any field, but its traditional
meaning is of a grassland cut annually for hay. Riverside fields
prone to seasonal flooding were
especially suitable for hay crops
and were cultivated in strips over
1,000 years ago by commoners
of the manor. They were known
as Lammas meadows because
commoners were forbidden to
graze animals in them between
Candlemas (February 2nd) and
Lammas Day (August 1st). Such
meadows are now rare, but once

had an astonishingly rich flora. Powick Hams have long since been drained and are now sown with rye-grass to provide rich grazing for livestock.

The path alongside the Teme eventually meets a weir where unusual plants such as green figwort and round-fruited rush grow with hemlock, purple loosestrife and tansy. In summer, swallows, house martins and swifts feed on emerging insects and give excellent opportunities for identification. Among them will be sand martins, brown hole-nesting birds which breed in the steep banks of the Teme. Mute swans are often in attendance, white adults trailing a flotilla of grey cygnets. These birds are now increasing in the county thanks partly to the banning of lead weight usage by anglers and largely to the efforts of the Swan Rescue group at Wychbold, who receive over 80% of Worcestershire's swans into their care each year. Bats too, frequent these waters. On summer evenings Daubenton's bats skim the river surface for insects; they roost by day in the curious brick chimney nearby, rumoured to be the first hydro-electric scheme in Britain.

Well signposted paths direct you on a circuit around the Hams, eventually leading up a steep bank at Ham Hill. Follow the yellow arrows back to the east and you reach Powick village. The county council and Severn Trent Water have placed benches at viewpoints to Worcester city and native trees have been planted to supplement existing varieties. Best of all, two pools have been created and are already being colonised by the scarce ruddy darter dragonfly. Five minute's walking will take you to Powick and the busy A449. Turn left at the butcher's and you soon regain your starting point. The entire walk covers less than two miles but if you wish to travel further you can follow the riverside path through to Bransford two miles on.

Before you leave the area, take time to visit the old three-arched sandstone bridge. Here in 1642 was the first Worcestershire skirmish of the Civil War. A cargo of silver plate from Oxford University escorted by Royalist dragoons arrived at Worcester en route for Aberystwyth mint. The dragoon leader, Sir John Byron, believing Parliamentarians were at hand, sent for assistance in the shape of Prince Rupert. The Parliamentarians, under the Earl of Essex thought that a Royalist army was assembling and attacked with a small expeditionary cavalry under Colonel Fiennes. They were easily subdued and retired to Powick Bridge where they attempted to surprise Prince Rupert's troops advancing to meet them. A short but savage battle left all Royalists but Rupert dead or wounded and fifty Parliamentarians were killed or drowned. Both sides claimed a victory! The full story of Worcester's involvement in the Civil wars is rivetingly told at The Commandery Civil War Centre at Sidbury - well worth a visit after your stroll at Powick.

Stonehall and Kempsey Commons

OSL Map 150
GR SO 882/485

OSP SO 84/94

East of M5 Motorway on minor roads south of Norton and west of Kempsey village.

Open grassland and gorse scrub with views to the Malvern Hills. Good flat walking at all seasons.

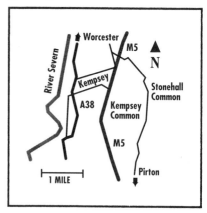

Public transport: Bus from Worcester via Kempsey. Alight south of Kempsey and walk up minor road to Napleton. Cross M5 to Kempsey Common.

Your only hint of the existence of these adjacent commons is from the M5 motorway. Drivers heading south from Worcester in high vehicles will catch a brief glimpse of gorsy grassland to the east where the road has impinged on the solitude. To visit these areas requires a little persistence and a good map, preferably the O/S Pathfinder series.

The easiest access is from Norton, signposted from the new Worcester by-pass. Follow the signs to Stonehall, where the common is immediately recognisable as a typical Worcestershire "waste", a strip of tussocky grass

hugging the road for half a mile and bordered by a huddle of cottages. Mark its pub well - you may need its services on a hot summer's day. There is little to search for on the common itself, though its hedgerow black pear-trees are a local speciality, relics of wider fruit-growing. However, at the southern end of the road a bridleway veers off into the gorse and through a gate onto the eastern edge of Kempsey Common.

On the Pathfinder maps, this is shown as the typical semi-circles of dots which indicate rough ground or heath. If you expect either feature you will be disappointed. Kempsey Common is a landscape pared to the bone. Go in May, the best time of all, and you will see four constituents - gorse, grass, sky and sheep. The grass has been nibbled almost to submission, but does contain a

102

scatter of plants including blinks and sheep's-sorrel. Dark banks of common gorse adorn the southern slopes beyond which motorway traffic roars dully, a constant drone which is almost soothing. Less soothing are the military aircraft which hurtle across at regular intervals; no matter how often they appear you are never quite ready for the ear-splitting sound of their passage.

Gorse is an under-rated shrub, an excellent nest-site for birds and a greenhouse speciality in what used to be Russia. May sees the bushes erupt in a blaze of golden blossom, superb against the backcloth of the Malvern Hills. Linnets, long-tailed tits and whitethroats all benefit from its spiny security and can be seen at several spots on the common.

Your route is dictated by the rights of way, though these are unclear on the ground and you are unlikely to be challenged (unless you have a free-ranging dog). A leisurely circuit takes around an hour, though you may wish to extend your walk to include Kempsey and Green Street or even the man-made Pirton Pool to the south.

Monkwood

OSL Map 150
GR SO 804/606 (car park)

OSP SO 86/96

Along minor road one mile from Sinton Green.

WNCT/BC. Ancient semi-natural wood. Flat paths with general access. Monkwood Green is to the south, a small common with ponds and flower-rich grassland.

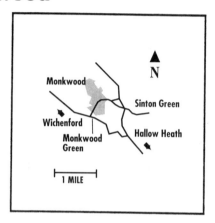

Public Transport: MRW 310 312 313

Travel west from the villages of Hallow or Sinton Green and, after a mile or two, you will reach Monkwood. It lies on a flat plain overlying Keuper marl soils and its survival in the midst of rich agricultural land indicates its past importance as a source of timber for surrounding settlements. At any season it is a wood to savour, easy to reach and with no gradients.

Monkwood was purchased by the WNCT in 1986 and is now managed in conjunction with the British Butterfly Conservation Society, now called Butterfly Conservation. Anyone familiar with "Harrised" woods will recognise the woodscape, a grid of narrow paths and tunnels between planta-

tions of beech, sycamore, birch and oak, grown to the right thickness for turning into brush handles. When the Trust acquired the wood, it was neglected, shot through with introduced trees. Rides had become choked with foliage, and butterflies and other sun-loving insects had been forced to the woodland edge, marginalised by the dense shade.

Now, thanks to careful management, Monkwood has been revived and is a popular walking place. Coppicing has resumed, rides have been widened and stone-chipped and a car-park has been built. A woodland map showing principal routes is here along with regularly updated sightings of wildlife.

This is a very old wood indeed. The Worcestershire historian, Dr. Pamela Gough, has traced the first record of the name to 1240, but there were trees here in 1086 at the time of the Domesday Book. Prior to that date it is likely that the area has never been cleared since the last Ice Age over 8,000 years ago. Its sinuous outline betrays its ancient beginnings - no modern plantation boasts such curves and inlets.

Stroll slowly through the trees in spring, and you can sense the antiquity. There are no forest giants, no hollow hulks, but a rich carpet of wild flowers. This is still haphazard, thriving best in new coppice where violets and primroses flourish, to be replaced with magenta spikes of betony in July.

The rarest plants are the hardest to find, but, search carefully beneath the gloom of the beeches and you will see the delicate bells of lily-of-the-valley emerging in May from a scabbard of green leaves.

Monkwood is best known for its butterflies. Over thirty species, half the British total, have been recorded, though some are distinctly rare. Small tortoiseshells, red admirals and fiery orange commas are frequent, but the two specialities are much less sensational in appearance. The first to emerge is the wood white which can be seen in early summer fluttering feebly along sunny rides.

Wood White

105

Local anywhere in Britain, it relies on undisturbed habitats and lacks the brashness of the two "cabbage whites". By contrast, the second beauty is a magnificent flier. White admirals soar and glide around open coppice performing feats of aerial agility that few other butterflies can match. Keeping them here is a delicate balance for, while the adults enjoy the sun, white admiral caterpillars feed on honeysuckle which grows best in the tangled shade of dense mature coppice.

Away from the central ride leading north from the car-park, the paths are wet even in high summer. The perimeter route offers a pleasant walk with tempting avenues branching regularly into the woodland heart. In autumn meadow saffron blooms pallidly and wild service seems to be everywhere, raining red and gold leaves onto the rides. If you prefer a longer walk, Ockeridge Wood lies to the north along a public footpath, while to the immediate south is the superb common of Monkwood Green.

Monkwood Green

Worcestershire is well-blessed with commons, large and small, but few are as attractive as this 17 acre green. On a map it is inconspicuous, tacked onto the larger wood like an afterthought, but drive out on the minor roads from Hallow or Grimley and you will discover a slice of countryside rich in history.

Most of the features of a traditional common can be found here- an abundance of rough grazing, small pools for watering livestock and a pub, the Fox Inn, which is a building in its place if ever there was one. Commoners' rights still attach to the land including turbary, which allows registered commoners to take turf, and estovers, a general right to gather underwood for fencing or burning. Footpaths across the green are few, but since it is owned by the local authority, you can wander anywhere.

In many ways this is a miniature version of the Malvern commons even down to the pollard willows and poplars around the tiny ponds. Hay is cut by local farmers, keeping the grass short and rich in flowers and insects. Gorse and heather thrive in the somewhat acid soil along with such meadow specialities as pepper saxifrage, neither a pepper or a saxifrage but an yelllow parsley blooming in July and August. Dyer's greenweed grows here too, its sulphur sprays of pea flowers perversely turning green as they dry. A clear yellow dye obtained from this plant is the basis of Kendal Green, blue wool often being "greened" by its application. Rarest of all the common's plants is petty whin, a diminutive gorse-like shrub. Its chrome-yellow flowers wreathed in spines appear in early summer and can only be seen at one other Worcestershire site, also an ancient common. Find it and you have found a fitting symbol for the county's declining commonlands.

Although the views of the Malverns are good, especially at sundown, you need little time to explore the green. However it makes an excellent starting point for a tour of Monkwood itself.

Hartlebury Common

OSL Map 138 GR SO
825/705

OSP SO 87/97

Car Parks. Wilden Top SO
827/715

A 4025 SO 821/704

*On A4025 and B4193 east
of Stourport on Severn, one
mile from town centre.*

*HWCC. Sandy heath ideal
for picnics and walking.
Excellent wildlife and views
across Severn Valley.
Guided walks programme
by rangers.*

*Public Transport: Buses
from Stourport.*

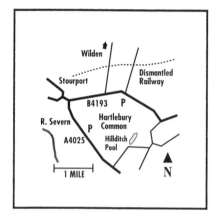

Ancient hippopotamus bones, delicate bog-flowers which eat insects and a system of shifting sand dunes make Hartlebury Common unique among Worcestershire sites. Although the housing estates of Stourport march alongside the common's boundaries, this astonishing place still manages to amaze its visitors.

In the 19th Century few county naturalists seem to have passed by without bestowing fulsome praise. Edwin Lees, the eminent botanist, described the common as:

"A waste of incoherent sand similar to a sea beach meets the view, diversified with bogs and pools nourishing many rarities, while the rising ground eastward forms a thick scrub of heather that might be worthy of any heath in Scotland"

The best place to begin your exploration of the common is the car-park at Wilden Top where the County Council's Countryside Service have placed information boards. Here gorse and heather dominate, though often blackened patches of heath signify unscheduled fires. Hollows in the ground are remnants of sand and gravel diggings in the late 19th and early 20th Centuries.

From the car park a bridleway leads south towards a plantation of Corsican pines, their sombre geometry incongruous in the soft landscape. They were planted in the early 1950's by schoolchildren to promote awareness of the countryside!

Take care as you tread the pathways across the common for they are home to the bizarre minotaur beetle which can be seen in spring stumbling myopically across the short turf. This three-horned beetle lays its eggs in rabbit droppings and is now a rare sight in the county.

The view to the west now reveals that the common is on two levels, Upper and Lower Terrace. From the scarp of Upper Terrace, the lower level resembles a piece of parchment in negative, cracked into a mosaic of paths which show up red against the liver-brown heather. Descending this slope is a tricky business, but it was much more dangerous for Victorian walkers who had to face a fusillade of ammunition from the firing range. To this day, a large sandy crater remains uncolonised by vegetation as evidence and is pinpricked with the holes of caterpillar-hunting sand wasps.

Near the A 4025 which crosses the lower terrace along the course of the old turnpike are pockets of water-retentive clay.

Worcestershire's only acid bog was thus created and core samples have revealed pollen trapped in the peat from 10,000 years ago, showing that the common was once pine-clad. Hippopotamus bones were also discovered, but the bog no longer shelters such exotic occupants. However, a rich collection of plants include the insectivorous sundew and cotton-grass. Rope-walks were once in operation nearby and the pool that remains was probably used as a retting pond to separate the hemp fibres prior to twisting into ropes.

Now the bog is in danger of drying out and is carefully managed by the rangers of the Countryside Service to prevent tree colonisation.

Lower Terrace is subject to a great deal of disturbance and its wildlife is limited. A few pairs of meadow pipits breed and very occasionally stonechats have summered, sounding their flinty calls from the gorse tops.

Hartlebury Common is part of the new Leapgate Country Park which includes a three-mile stretch of disused railway line and Hillditch Pool. Once more open in aspect, the pool lies in a wooded valley once known poetically as Vallombrosa. Large carp glide in its waters, while terrapins provide an unexpected sight on hot days. Dumped by a pet-shop owner, they have grown fat at the expense of the local ecosystem.

A path follows the pool, then leads into a marshy dingle, emerging in a narrow lane. Turn left and you reach Hartlebury Castle, home of the Bishop of Worcester and of the County Museum.

Shrawley Wood

OSL Map 150
GR SO 800/658 (Rose and
Crown Inn)

OSP S0 86/96
GR SO 798/663 (New Inn)

Off B4196 two miles south
of Astley Cross, near Stourport.

Private/FC. Splendid
ancient woodland noted for
its lime coppice and bluebells. Well-served with
paths and with access to
the Severn. Generally flat
with a few slopes and river
scarp.

Public transport: Bus service from Stourport. MRW
293 and 294.

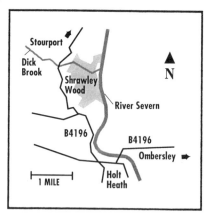

The signs which appear every
May outside Shrawley village hall
advertising "Bluebell Walks" are
the only hint that woods are
nearby. At other seasons potential visitors could drive through
the straggling two-mile village and
miss 500 acres of glorious ancient
woodland.

Although it lies hidden, sandwiched between the B4196 and
the River Severn, access is not a
problem, merely a matter of finding the right spots. The two most
convenient footpaths are, provi-
dentially, opposite pubs. At the

north end of the village, the path
enters the wood across the road
from the New Inn, next to the
post office. A mile further south is
the Rose and Crown opposite a
bridleway which leads into the
wood by Layes Pool. Ask at either
pub and the landlords are sure to
oblige with a parking place in return for a little patronage after
your walk. Non-drinkers can
enjoy the sandy bridleway leading
south from Astley Burf. If you are
planning a circular route it is useful to remember that the B4196
has no footpath and that vehicles
travel fast around its many bends.

Paths around the wood are many,
but unsurfaced, and the standard
warnings about squelchy surfaces
apply in wet weather.

Without doubt Shrawley's finest
features are its small-leaved limes,
a relic of the original woodland

110

which covered large areas of Worcestershire 5000 years ago. Pollen samples, which remain identifiable for thousands of years, show that lime was one of the commonest trees in southern and midland England. Its subsequent decline was due partly to clearance of the wildwood, as Oliver Rackham has called it, in Neolithic and Bronze Age periods and partly to climatic change. Lime was the last of our native trees to hop aboard before Britain cast loose from mainland Europe and still has trouble germinating from seed. Finger-leaved seedlings sprout regularly in Shrawley,but nearly all perish by their second year.

To see limes at their best in one of the best limewoods in England, enter the wood opposite the Rose and Crown. Here, huge coppiced trunks or poles arise from stools centuries old. Coppicing has been practised for generations producing fifty-foot lengths of virtually grain-free white timber; an old county name for the tree is "whitewood". Even the bark had a use, the fibrous inner lining yielding a string known as "bast".

In this part of the wood, limes are dominant. They once occupied a much larger area but were replaced in the post-war forestry boom by the inevitable conifers. Now the Forestry Commission have a more enlightened stance regarding old woods and it is likely that the limes will survive. Over 250 acres, partly in private ownership, have been designated a SSSI. In winter lime twigs glow red like capillaries, seventy feet above the forest floor. In spring the heart-shaped foliage casts a filigreed shade over thousands of bluebells, hence the advertised walks. Anyone who curses our wet and unpredictable Atlantic climate, can take comfort in the huge numbers of bluebells which throng British woodlands. East of Germany, it is simply too cold and dry. The hanging flowers beg to be picked, but soon die in water. They no longer have a use, but in the 16th century the "slimie, glewish juice" was recorded by the herbalist Gerard as a paper paste. Carpets as extensive as this take hundreds of years to grow so to stand in Shrawley beneath a canopy of lime is an unforgettable experience.

Spring sees the wood fill up with birds. Garden warblers and willow warblers breed in the newly-cut coppice, giving way to chiffchaffs and woodpeckers as the trees mature. Occasionally, pied flycatchers sing in the huge oaks, whose companions were felled to provide panelling for the House of Commons after damage in World War II. Follow any path for long enough and you meet the ride which divides the wood. It is dominated by two towering redwoods, visible for miles around. These enormous conifers have spongy bark which you can punch without harming yourself and which provides winter insulation for roosting treecreepers. At each end of the ride the paths lead downhill to the Severn. To the south are the sandstone outcrops of Oliver's Mound, which may once have been inhabited by hermits. These, so legend claims, rescued infants cast adrift on the river and raised them, giving the adopted foundlings the surname Severn.

A riverside walk leads north across the Shrawley Brook to Hamstall and Astley Burf or south past old clay-diggings to Lenchford. All routes within the wood return to the B4196, so keep within the trees and you will not lose your way.

Chaddesley Wood

OSL Map 139
GR SO 914/736

OSP SO 87/97

On minor road from A448 at Wardcote Green.

English Nature. Ancient semi-natural oak woodland with some conifer plantation. Rich in wildlife. Good and flat walking in all weathers.

Most of path suitable for wheelchairs, but stile at beginning is an unfortunate obstacle.

Public transport: Bus along A448 Bromsgrove to Kidderminster.

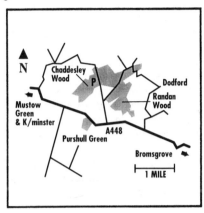

Little-known except by locals, yet surprisingly easy to reach, Chaddesley Woods form a block of ancient oak woodland on the loamy clays between Bromsgrove and Kidderminster. Although there are several coppices, the only accessible area is Chaddesley itself, where Nature Conservancy Council(now English Nature) opened the Jubilee Walk in 1977 to mark the 25th Anniversary of Queen Elizabeth II. The complete system of woods was declared a National Nature Reserve four years earlier since it is a classic example of lowland oakwood and shelters a rich and varied flora and fauna.

Sadly the list no longer includes wild boar and wolves, though you may be secretly grateful for this. Royal hunting parties once sought their quarry here when Chaddesley was part of the Royal Forest of Feckenham. Following the Norman Conquest, this vast tract of land extended across most of north-east Worcestershire. Not all was woodland - hunting rights covered open fields, heaths and commons and the prey seems positively exotic by modern standards. Wild cats, martens and red deer were all pursued vigorously so perhaps it is hardly surprising that all are extinct in the county today.

Feckenham Forest was largely denuded of timber in the early 17th Century, felled to provide fuel for the burgeoning Black Country industries. Remaining fragments are doubly precious, a living link with the Middle Ages.

The Jubilee Walk is short and circular. You can stroll around it in a brisk half-hour, but that would be a pity. Slow down and the rewards are many. English Nature provide free trail guides from dispensers at the entrance, but are less considerate about cars. Parking is limited in the narrow lane, so please take care not to block the ride entrance.

Oak and sallows, the pussy-willow of school nature tables, line the first section of the walk, a wide avenue alive with flickering butterflies. High summer sees the emergence of wasp-coloured longhorn beetles from years of imprisonment as fat,white grubs in rotting wood. Commercial forestry has no place for dead timber-or longhorn beetles.

Oak is popularly said to support 284 species of insect. Most have little noticeable effect on their host plant, but one,the oak tortrix can be devastatingly obvious. Huge numbers of tiny green caterpillars attack the leaves reducing them to tattered skeletons. When such plagues occur flocks of tits and starlings swarm in to reap the bounty. The oaks compensate by producing a second flush of red-tinged foliage known as Lammas growth because it appears around Lammas Day, the old harvest festival on August 1st.

South of the oakwoods conifers hold sway. These modern planta-

tions are incongruous in ancient woodland, but English Nature have retained them as a comparison with the broadleaves. It is easy to criticise large-scale coniferisation and much is unforgivable, but in Chaddesley the pines and larches add to the diversity. Our smallest bird, the goldcrest sings its needling song here. In favourable years crossbills turn up. You can detect them by their chipping calls or by the shower of pine seeds which surround you as you stand beneath a feeding flock.

If a foul stench, as of rotting carrion assails you on this section, you are probably standing near a stinkhorn. These rocket-shaped fungi burst from a white "egg" and are initially coated with an evil-smelling mucus containing spores. Flies attracted by the taint of putrefaction land on the slime and spread the spores on their feet.

A grove of young coast redwoods, fiery bark glowing against the pines marks a fork in the path by a badgers' sett. You are unlikely to see the animals, but their presence can be detected by excavations of sand, deposited on this higher part of the wood by glacial meltwater thousands of years ago. Badger are more frequent in the county than for many years despite the barbarous attentions of diggers. This is a well-watched sett and is unlikely to be persecuted.

Past the sett the path drops steeply to the right to skirt a

114

poplar grove. Rustlings in the undergrowth may betray the whereabouts of muntjac, retriever-sized deer introduced to England at Woburn Abbey Around 1900. Linger late and you can hear the bucks barking or see them crossing rides. They visit local gardens and prove a pest nibbling roses.

From here the path curls gently back to the main ride. While you are in the area, Chaddesley Corbett village is well worth a visit. Its church is the only one in England dedicated to Saint Cassian who was stabbed to death by the pens of ungrateful pupils. The 12th Century font attracted the attention of no less than Sir John Betjeman who described the church as the "best example of 14th Century work in the county".

Purshull Green

OSL Map
139 GR SO 900/715

OSP SO 87/97

On minor roads, south of A448 near Chaddesley Corbett.

Section 9 Common. Open dairy grassland in farmland. Pools and small settlements. Ideal for a short walk or for access to Chaddesley Wood. Flat but muddy in places at all seasons. Wheelchair access along no through road leading to the green.

Public Transport. Bus along A448 Bromsgrove to Kidderminster.

This is definitely not a place you will find by accident - it needs to be hunted down, but is well worth the effort. To get there travel east on the A448 Kidderminster Bromsgrove road. Beyond Chaddesley Corbett village, take the second turn on the right where a signpost directs you to Elmbridge. About a mile along this tree-fringed lane is a left turning to Purshull Green; the entrance to the common is marked by a public bridleway sign a few hundred yards on. Parking is limited, but if you wish you can drive along the metalled bridleway for a short distance.

The approach is less than inspiring, an unfenced road lined with broad grassy verges and liberally scattered with agricultural machinery, some operational, some not. Smallholdings abound and there are odd concealed pools, their margins stomped bare by sheep and cattle. In spite of this, they are the breeding grounds of several species of dragonfly and damselfly. Eventually the path splits to enclose a large willow-fringed pond next to Elm Farm. Mallards and Canada geese breed here and chestnut-faced little grebes whinny from the rushes. The bridleway leads to the right, past Pool House Farm (no trades descriptions problems there!) and alongside a new red-brick house not yet marked on the maps. Immediately beyond is the largest area of grassland, a modest meadow full of tufted hair grass. It looks good for picnickers, but can be damp at any season and there are the added hazards of woolly thistles whose leaves sprawl across the turf like enormous thorny starfish. To stand here on an autumn evening is to experience the intimate, almost fey atmosphere of the place. Hedged about with oaks whose ancestors graced the Royal Forest of Feckenham, the green is an amazing survivor in a predominantly arable landscape.

The path leads eventually into an old orchard where little owls bob on fence-posts and old plum trees lean drunkenly. Follow the stiles for ten minutes or so and you reach the A448 at Woodhouse Farm. For a longer walk, cross the road and follow the bridleway into Chaddesley Wood and the Jubilee Walk.

Pepper Wood

OSL Map 139
GR SO938/744

OSP SO 87/97

On minor road west of Bournheath.

Woodland Trust. Ancient semi-natural oak woodland, now coppiced. Many paths through trees and central ride suitable for wheelchairs.

Public Transport: Bus from Bromsgrove to Fairfield.

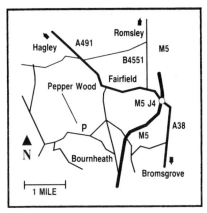

Welcome to Britain's first community woodland.From the moment you enter the small car-park, Woodland Trust signs greet you, insurance enough that this wood at least is in safe ownership. Not only are there the usual map, facts and figures, but right from the start you are given an opportunity to get involved by joining a working party.

For Pepper is no ordinary woodscape - it works for its living and is probably the nearest we get in the 20th century to a medieval coppice. Local volunteers manage the wood for its timber and wildlife, and in the process have created a superb habitat for people too. You can enjoy its attractions on many levels - walk the dog, admire the flowers or shed a few pounds coppicing the birch and hazel. It seems a novel concept in our urban mechanised age - woodland as factory and community centre.

Of course, it's not a new idea at all, merely re-cycled. In the Middle Ages, Pepper Wood was a vital lifeline for nearby villages, providing wood for burning and fencing and timber for building. Different thicknesses were obtained by coppicing. All British broad-leaved trees sprout again when cut, a phenomenon which Oliver Rackham, the woodland historian, has dubbed "constant spring". This ability to re-grow means that woods are difficult to destroy, though none will survive the onslaught of bulldozers. By cutting sections of a wood on cycles of say, five, ten or twenty years, villagers could obtain all the material they needed. A number of trees were left to mature to provide tall straight timber for house construction.

Commercial forestry from the 19th Century onwards put an end to traditional practices and Pepper Wood, which had been a model coppice, became a neglected tangle. In the 1940's it was largely clear-felled but the fabric remained intact, allowing the Woodland Trust to begin a new regime following their purchase of the area in 1981. Now

the wood has its own sales manager from whom you can buy fence-posts of durable oak, hedging stakes and bean-poles of hazel and birch besoms. Prices are keen, but even these cannot compete with an entire oak sold in 1262 for the equivalent of 8.5p.

A few paces along the excellent trail gives the flavour of Pepper Wood. This is a light, airy place with open, newly-coppiced clearings. Cut wood is stacked in parallel "hedges", any not used creat-

Coppicing as it used to be

118

ing a refuge for wildlife. A stone-chip bridleway, suitable for wheelchairs, bisects the wood. Sinuous paths cross it, offering plenty of scope for exploration. Off the bridleway, these become muddy after rain, but walking conditions are generally good and gradients gentle.

To the east of the car-park the soil is remarkably acid, favouring bilberries. In the shade they seldom produce a crop, but in open glades are more forthcoming. A distinctive flower here is common cow-wheat which bears yellow, snapdragon blooms and is semi-parasitic on the roots of grasses.

Birds, especially warblers thrive in coppice. Stand on the fringe of an open glade in summer and you will hear the contralto bubblings of garden warblers, plain grey-brown relatives of the blackcap. Sparrowhawks often soar over the clearings on taut, barred wings, prospecting for prey which they pursue in a madcap slalom between the tree trunks.

Old coppice regimes encourage plants and butterflies, revelling in the dappled interplay of sun and shade. Brimstones - the original "butter-coloured fly"- appear in early spring after a seven-month sleep in an ivy cluster. Sheets of bluebells and white stitchwort lap against oak trunks in May, increasing along rides or newly felled areas. West of the main bridleway is a grove of oak, birch and rowan left to grow on as high forest. Here you will find those faithful indicators of ancient woodland, small-leaved lime and wild service. Autumn sees the trees filled with fussing parties of tits, treecreepers and nuthatches, with, if you are lucky, the occasional bonus of a lesser spotted woodpecker.

Pepper Wood takes its name from Pyppa, the father of Penda, a king of 7th Century Mercia. With continuing care, it may well yet resemble the woodscape he knew.

119

Trench Wood

OSL Map 150
GR SO 929/589

OSP SO 85/95

Along minor roads south of B4090 2 miles east of Droitwich.

WNCT. Ancient woodland rich in wildlife. Good network of flat paths, but many muddy at all seasons.

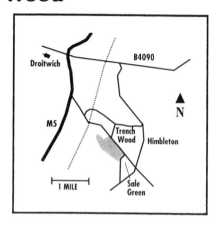

A wood best experienced in semi-darkness for just six weeks of the year sounds less than promising, but nothing could be further from the truth. Trench wood, near Huddington is a jewel in the crown of the WNCT and rightly so, for it harbours some of the finest woodland wildlife in the county. Tucked deep in the maze of lanes south of the old Salt Way, along which salt was once transported from Droitwich brine pits, it is a chunk of ancient woodland well worth exploring. There are actually three woods comprising Trench, two known collectively as "The Trenches" and Popeshill Wood, which is bordered by a ditch and woodbank. Find such a feature and you have strong evidence of medieval coppice, managed woodland which would be protected from wandering livestock by the construction of an uncrossable barrier. This one has a double significance for

it also marks the parish boundary.

As you soon see when entering the wood from Trench Lane, there are few old trees in sight. The main area is a private enclave to the north-west, where century-old oaks loom over neglected hazel coppice and early purple orchids bloom in deep shade. Elsewhere, younger trees grow in blocks of equal age, forming dense thickets of sycamore, grey alder, birch and beech. Between the plantations is a grid of shaded paths and rides, lush and cool even in mid-summer. Few of these trees are more than twenty feet high which gives a clue to the wood's previous ownership. When The Harris Brush company re-planted the wood over thirty years ago with fast-growing white timber suitable for turning into brush handles, they unwittingly created the perfect habitat for the doyen of England's songbirds - the nightingale.

Hence the need for darkness and six weeks in late spring. Nightingales arrive in late April from their winter quarters in West Africa and are attracted to the dense coppice. In Worcestershire they reach their north-western limits and appear to be declining. Males arrive first and begin singing by day and night to entice potential mates.

Few wildlife experiences can match the thrill of stepping into Trench Wood late on a windless May evening. As the chorus of warblers and thrushes thins, woodcocks begin their curious territorial circuits. Moths blunder across the rides and a chill mist seeps into the damper corners of the wood. Suddenly, without warning, the nightingales start up, staccato bursts of pure liquid notes which cannot be mistaken for any other birdsong. These are not the mellifluous warbling of blackbirds, but short and intensely sweet phrases, some ending abruptly in a glottal stop, and some punctuated by rich spells of "jugging" for which the birds are renowned. Even the pauses between song - phrases are expertly timed, allowing you to savour the last stanza. The performers are rarely seen, skulking deep within the undergrowth - get too close and they melt into the foliage with a warning growl.

Understandably, the wood is popular between late April and early June, and there is even some

danger of over-disturbance. You will hear and see more if you keep to the main rides and do not move about too much. Paths in the wood are often sticky with clay even in summer and many are narrow and overgrown, However, the size of the area prevents you from getting lost. Dawdling is heartily recommended if you wish to find the choicest plants. June sees the appearance of sweet-smelling greater butterfly orchids along the rides while in spring the green-flowered herb, paris, blooms unobtrusively throughout the coppice. This indicator of ancient woodland has no connections with the French capital, but derives its name from the Latin for "equal". All parts of the plant are symmetrical, from the four-leaved rosette to the eight stamens and strange green petals. The plant is poisonous, though its twinned leaves have inevitably led to a folklore of true lovers paired until eternity.

The WNCT work hard to maintain the wood in optimum condition for wildlife, preserving the delicate balance favoured by the nightingales and other birds and plants. If you enjoy your visit, please remember that the wood and its superb natural history were purchased as a result of public donations - every little helps and the whole site could easily have been lost forever.

Less than a mile to the south-east is Huddington Court, one of the finest 16th century timber-framed buildings in the county. Here in 1605, its owners, Thomas and

Robert Winter conspired with their cousin Robert Catesby to blow up James the First's Parliament. The Gunpowder Plot failed and after Guy Fawkes was captured, they fled to Stourbridge, but were arrested and executed for treason. Lady Winter's ghost is said to walk the grounds, restlessly awaiting Thomas and Robert's return. The house is privately owned, but may be viewed from the public footpath.

Piper's Hill

OSL Map 150
GR SO 958/650

OSP SO 86/96

Along B4091 south of Bromsgrove and north of Hanbury.

Private. Wooded hilltop with old beeches and chestnuts. Good dry walking with footpaths to Hanbury Hall.

Public transport: MRW 141 stops at Avoncroft Museum 2 miles to the north.

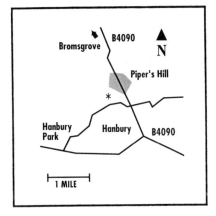

The motorist travelling south from Bromsgrove on the Hanbury road across Piper's Hill could be excused for imagining himself in the Chilterns. This is a woodscape virtually unknown elsewhere in Worcestershire - huge beeches shade the highway and the cool depths of the wood are irresistible. So, why resist? Pull off the road and explore this fascinating area.

On closer examination, Piper's Hill has many features of ancient wood-pasture. Most of the magnificent beeches and sweet chestnuts have been pollarded to allow wood to be cropped and livestock to be grazed beneath. This practice which was already well-established at the time of the Domes-day Book, prevented regeneration of saplings, leading to open, airy woods and fine specimen trees.

And what trees! Beside the smooth-trunked beeches, the most dramatic hulks here are the chestnuts, massive boles twisted as if they had been given a "Chinese burn" by a vast, anonymous hand. Neither species is native here or indeed anywhere else in the county, but are nonetheless popular with hole-nesting birds. Great spotted woodpeckers flash black-and-white between the trunks and bandit-masked nuthatches wolf-whistle from the rotten branches.

Not all the tree-dwellers are birds. Look carefully at each nest-hole and you may spot the dark urine-stains which betray the roost site of noctules. Our largest common bats, they emerge at dusk to hawk for moths and beetles high over the wood.

There is no need here for a "Please do not pick the flowers" sign - there are hardly any. The dense shade of the beeches and the dry glacial drift deposits are unfavourable to most woodland plants. However, there is one curious plant which offers research opportunities for the patient seeker. Bird's-nest orchids bloom in June in the deepest gloom, deriving their sustenance from rotting timber and leaves. The brown flower-spikes are as unlike the traditional orchid image as you could imagine, and blend perfectly with their russet backcloth.

Away from the noisy road the paths border agricultural land. For a longer visit, you may like to take the footpath to the south-west, exploring Hanbury church and the grounds of Hanbury Hall beyond. Now owned by the National Trust, the elegant Queen Anne house was given away by its last owner, Sir George Vernon, to the daughter of his estate foreman.

The Eastern Fringe

Not always to explore, the south-east of Worcestershire is the domain of agriculture. The fertile Vale of Evesham, famous for its fruit-growing, surrounds the River Avon and occupies much of the flatter ground. Easily accessible open spaces are generally confined to the fringing Oolitic hills of the Cotswolds above Broadway and the massive dome of Bredon Hill which gives superb views across Gloucestershire and the "straits of Malvern".

Arrow Valley Country Park

Feckenham Wylde Moor

Cleeve Prior
Windmill Hill

Broadway Gravel Pit
Fish Hill Picnic Site
Broadway Tower

Tiddesley Wood

Bredon Hill

Arrow Valley Park

OSL 150 Car Parks: GR SP 065/678 North

OSP SP 06/16
GR SP 061/664 Ipsley Pool

Along A428 and B4497 in Redditch

RBC. Mixture of fields, wood and pools with large angling and sailing lake. Good metalled paths and walks throughout.

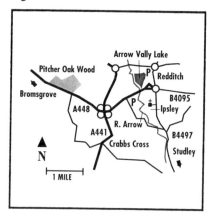

Public Transport: Buses from Birmingham and Bromsgrove to Redditch.

Purists will no doubt argue that there is no place for Redditch in a guide to the Worcestershire countryside - after all this New Town which burgeoned in the 1970s and 1980s occupies large tracts of the county previously "unspoilt", the euphemism so close to the hearts of estate agents and tourist authorities.

You find it here because, however managed and manufactured its landscape, Arrow valley is, above all, accessible. The Park's variety of habitats and opportunities is unsurpassed in the surrounding "unspoilt" farmland and there is a welcome absence of "Keep Out" signs. There's no need to ask if this plantation or that field is out of bounds - it isn't. Furthermore

there are signboards at every carpark detailing main features so that getting lost is virtually impossible. In spite of this apparent order, Redditch Borough Council has retained enough rough areas to allow the inquisitive to fossick about in the quieter ditches and dingles.

Unless you live there, navigating through Redditch is a nightmare. Miss one turn on the intestinal coils of its road system and you could be in for a long detour. Ironically, the town is built on the Ryknild Way, a Roman road which borders the park to the east. Roman engineers would be horrified were they to witness the contortions of the modern network. Furthermore Arrow Valley Park is poorly signposted, so it is best to make for the north carpark at Church Hill or that next to Ipsley Mill Pool. This last site is the quieter, with stone-chipped paths, ditches lined with bluebells and wild garlic and billowing hedges, redolent of the countryside. Only the orange life-belts provided by the Borough Council remind you that you are in town. Safety is the watchword - this is a "poop-scoop" zone as dog owners should note.

Between the dingles and pathways flows the River Arrow looking beguilingly rural - stretches of shingle and deep pools beckon to the keen angler, but fishing is forbidden. However one resident is exempt - few birds can produce the heart-stopping thrill of a kingfisher as it darts upstream leaving its after-image burning into the water. The banks of the Arrow are steep and sandy, ideal habitats for kingfisher nests. In mid-summer, the burrows can be detected by the seepage of fish-slime and excreta. Small wonder that these brilliant birds rarely have their eggs taken.

Banks of water figwort line the river. A tall herb with inconspicuous foxy flowers, it has winged stems and was once known to children as "fiddlestrings". Rub two stalks together and you will discover why - they produce a squeaky vegetable whining. It's doubtful whether any of the local children will have tried this, because they are too intent on cycling, horse-riding, playing games or one of the many other activities the park has to offer.

South of the A4189, the park is a fascinating motley of woods, sports grounds, plantations and tussocky fields alive in summer with willow warblers and whitethroats. To the north is Arrow Lake itself, man-made and with its own sailing club. Fishing is allowed here and there is a ranger service offering information and a guided walks programme. Encircled completely by paths and neatly-mown grassland, the lake is formal and raw, but the groves of willows planted on its banks should soften its outline. Resident Canada geese are certainly at home and beg shamefully for titbits.

From end to end, the Park is under two miles long, but is as varied and well-managed a piece of "rus-in-urbe" as you will find in the neighbouring countryside. An added attraction at the southern end is the well-signposted Forge Mill Museum, which chronicles Redditch's needle-making industry and hosts a wide range of visiting exhibitions.

Feckenham Wylde Moor

OSL Map 150
GR SP 011/603

OSP SP 06/16

Along unclassified no through road from B4090 at Feckenham.

WNCT. Lowland marsh with excavated pool and bird-watching guide. Paths very wet - strong shoes essential.

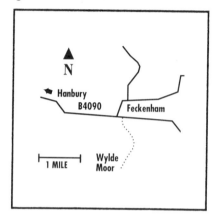

The rule "stout shoes in wet weather" applies to most Worcestershire sites, but Feckenham is different: for this one you'll need wellies all year round. And, while it's not the easiest of country, who could resist the allure of any place called a "wylde moor"?

Its location is the biggest surprise. Travel west from Hanbury along the old Salt Way through the village of Feckenham, and you will easily miss this WNCT reserve which lies at the bottom of Moors Lane. There are no clues in the surrounding countryside either, an unpromising expanse of dry pasture. To discover the moor, park in Feckenham village and cross the Roman road (the B4090) to join Moors Lane, a no-through road with few parking places. After about five minute's walking, the houses fade out and the lane drops into a network of hedges and fields. Willows appear to your

right and the reserve is marked by the Trust's house martin logo.

The first sight that confronts you is a magnificent wooden hide in which up to 16 people can survey the marsh and its wildlife. A pool has been excavated to encourage breeding birds and dragonflies for which the "wylde moor" is renowned. Recently tufted ducks have bred for the first time and this is a good place in which to make the acquaintance of ruddy ducks. When the first of these North Americans escaped from Slimbridge in the 1950s, bird-watchers had few inklings of its meteoric conquest of the English Midlands. Now the chestnut drakes with their impossibly bright-blue bills are found on many Worcestershire waters while the duller females skulk in waterside vegetation. Take your time in the hide - you may spot a rare ornithological gem such as a hunting hobby or, in the gloom of a December evening, a patrolling barn owl.

From the hide a trail skirts the edge of the moor, taking in the plants for which the marsh is famous. The underlying Lias clays trap water and rotting vegetation, producing sedgy peat. As you squelch around you can search for botanical highlights - marsh woundwort, blunt-flowered rush and maritime sea club-rush, unusual inland but flourishing here. Take care as you go to avoid the old drainage wells and ditches dug in the mid-19th century. They failed because the clay proved too efficient in trapping water.

A small, but expanding reed-bed is the only generally accessible one in the county and holds sedge and reed warblers in summer. Although the county has so many thatched dwellings, imported straw took precedence over locally grown reeds and so there was little incentive to retain them. Pits full of tea-brown water have been dug into the reeds to provide dragonflies with breeding sites. Among the species found here are the emperor, the four-spotted libellula and the black-tailed skimmer: unfortunately they hardly ever sit for long enough for you to identify them!

Cleeve Prior

OSL Map 150
GR SP 079/418

OSP SP 04/14

Along no-through woods to Avon west of B4085 in Cleeve Prior village.

HWCC. Riverside woodland with ridge-top walk and open grassland. Paths steep through woodland and muddy by river. Good access to Avon with walks to Offenham.

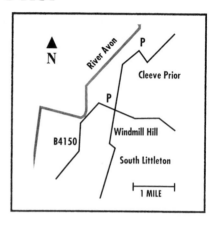

Perched on a limestone ridge 200 feet above the River Avon, Cleeve Prior is a nature reserve owned by the county council and managed by the WNCT. Though not a large area, it is an excellent access point for the river or for the ridge-top bridleway which continues south to Windmill Hill.

Parking is limited in Mill Lane, but Birmingham Anglers Association, who hold the fishing rights, have a private car-park at the riverside and are very accommodating outside the fishing season. Drive down to the river though, and you miss the reserve entrance on the left at the top of the hill. A cross-shaped stone, here since at least 1772 is traditionally supposed to mark the spot from which Prince Edward surveyed the site of the Battle of Evesham in 1265. The

stone now conceals the skeletons of several unfortunates uncovered nearby in 1824 and thought to be the remains of soldiers fleeing from the battlefield and drowned in the Avon.

Rank grassland along the bridleway gives way to scrub and ash woodland beloved of woodpeckers and turtle doves. These elegant chestnut-mantled birds are the essence of lazy summer days, crooning soporifically from the green depths of the hawthorn. The path is flanked by immense tufts of woolly thistle, a statuesque plant with huge trusses of purple blooms. This lover of lime flowers in July and can be identified by its arching leaves and buds thick with white "wool".

A few hundred yards on the path splits, the right hand fork leading down through trees to the river.

Budding Borgias would have a field day, for here grow two of our most deadly plants. Hemlock, infamous for polishing off Socrates, forms thickets at the water's edge. Its feathery leaves and umbels of white parsley-like flowers seem innocuous until you brush past and catch the mousy smell - definitely one to leave alone.

Lurking in the nearby scrub is a much rarer killer. Deadly nightshade has its only regular county site at Cleeve. Although the shiny black "Devil's Cherries" contain a fatal concoction, the plant was once grown commercially for the drug atropine, valued by oculists for dilating the pupils. This property has endowed the plant with the alternative name belladonna-"beautiful lady"- since it was used by women as a cosmetic to increase their pupil size and hence their allure.

Soon the path rejoins the river bank, offering a choice. Turn right and you return to the car-park. Narrow and steep, this route is cleared by fishermen, but can be very slippery in wet weather. Alternatively, for a circular walk of about three miles, turn left and head south along the river. In summer your constant companions are troupes of lustrous damselflies known as banded demoiselles. Arguably our most attractive insect, they are a metallic turquoise, each wing splashed with a navy ink-blot.

River traffic can be heavy along this stretch, and the lock here is one of nine along the Worcestershire Avon, built to control the water level. Past the lock and its associated water mill, the path bisects a caravan park to emerge on the B4510 conveniently close to the Fish & Anchor inn. To the left at the top of Windmill Hill, is a tree-lined bridleway leading north to Cleeve Prior and your starting point.

Windmill Hill

OSL Map 150
GR SP 072/477 (Parking)

OSP SP 04/14

Off B4510 between River Avon and North Littleton.

WNCT. Limestone grassland, rich in wild flowers. Good views across Avon to orchard country.

Windmill Hill is a spot to savour on two counts. First, it is one of the few areas of accessible open countryside in the Vale of Evesham and second, it is probably the best place to put yourself through a very pleasurable crash course in limestone flowers. All this and views too make it a must.

The 15 acre site was purchased in 1979 by the WNCT with help from the Countryside Commission and the World Wildlife Fund (as it was then). It consists largely of grassland and scrub to the east of the B4510 and is bordered by a bridle path. As soon as you reach the top of the road, you see the flowers spilling out onto the verge. Their survival, is due not to the whim of a sentimental farmer, but more practically to the steepness of the location. Windmill Hill is the southern end of a mile-long ridge of Rhaetic limestone shadowing the Avon flood plain and, unlike the surrounding landscape, has proved proved hard to cultivate.

Stiles lead from the bridleway into small fields which offer commanding views across the river terraces. To the south-west lies Evesham, encircled by orchards of apples and plums, while all around are glistening phalanxes of greenhouses, dazzling to the eye on sunny days. Peas, beans and beet are also grown on the fertile alluvial loam and even on the reserve, asparagus spears linger in the hedgerows as crop relics.

Every place has its season. On Windmill Hill this is late June or early July when the plants are at their best. Pink pyramidal orchids bloom along the open paths and salad burnet exudes a cucumber

scent when trodden underfoot. A very special plant is wild liquorice with broad acacia-like leaves providing a perfect counterpoint to its creamy pea's-blossoms. This is a scarce plant in Worcestershire, but you could be forgiven for thinking so having seen the luxuriant clumps dotted throughout the meadows or jostling for space in the hedge-bottoms. Such a profusion of plants has attracted 29 species of butterfly including the elegant marbled white. Day-flying moths include the curiously-named Mother Shipton. Christened after the famous Yorkshire prophetess, the insect bears the unmistakable hooked profile of a witch etched in white on its chocolate forewings.

Explore the hillside at leisure or rest and admire the splendid spire of Harvington church, green with oxide. Take care where you sit - the flat rosettes of stemless thistle are everywhere and it's not called "picnic" thistle for nothing!

If you prefer you can continue south to South Littleton or use Windmill Hill as the start of a circular walk to Cleeve Prior, returning along the river path to the Fish and Anchor public house.

Broadway Gravel Pit

OSL Map 150
GR SP 088/379

OSP SP 03/13

Along Childswickham Road off A46 at Broadway.

WNCT (leased from WDC) Gravel pit with adjoining land - nature trail and hide.

Public Transport: Bus from Evesham

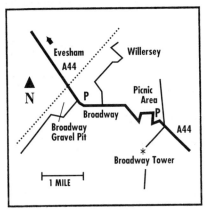

When you grow tired of the bustling streets of Broadway, of endless browsing for over-priced antiques and of searching for a place to park, look no further than this tiny oasis, a mere five minute's walk from the village centre. This reserve is leased by the WNCT from Wychavon District Council and is a valuable wildlife habitat in the dry Vale of Evesham, where any still water is rare indeed.

There is a small car-park near the railway bridge at Childswickham Road from which an iron gate leads onto a mini-trail. A hide for several people overlooks a shaded pool surrounded by statuesque white willows whose silver-backed leaves glisten in summer showers. Moorhens and mallards breed on the pool which also contains one of Worcestershire's two colonies of mare's-tail. Not to be confused

with the garden pest horsetail, this is an aquatic plant with stiff spikes of green leaves, rather like a bottle-brush. How it arrived here is uncertain; the pit is of recent origin, excavated to provide oolitic gravels washed from the Cotswolds by the Badsey Brook.

The hide makes a good shelter during rain when you can enter up your sightings in the log maintained by honorary wardens. In fine weather, you can explore the trail weaving between the willows. Dragonflies are common in high summer, the two most obvious being the red common darter and the dauntingly large southern hawker. This last species is black, bejewelled with blue and green and has the alarming habit of flying around you inquisitively. There is, of course, no need to be alarmed. Despite such names as devil's darning needle and horse-stinger, these beautiful insects are completely harmless.

In places the water has dried out and thistles and teasels have taken over. Butterflies are attracted to the flower-heads; brimstones, peacocks, commas and small tortoiseshells can all be seen near the hide. So, next time the tourists are too much, seek sanctuary at the gravel pit.

Fish Hill Picnic Site

OSL Map 150 GR SP 120/370

OSP SP 03/13

Off A44 at summit is Broadway Hill.

HWCC. Picnic area with benches, toilets, parking. Open grassland and woodland trail.

Public Transport: Bus from Evesham.

Foot travellers, usually drovers, plodding wearily up the limestone scarp behind Broadway were thirsty people when they reached the top. In fact, they drank like fishes at the summit inn, hence the hill's name. Now, cars power effortlessly through to the Cotswold heartland, ignoring the picnic site just off the main road. This is a pity, for the place makes a pleasant stopping-off point with the added bonus of a toposcope and a woodland walk.

Managed by HWCS, the picnic area lies on the boundary with Gloucestershire over the golden oolitic limestone. This, like that of Bredon Hill, was laid down during the Jurassic period and is the youngest of the county's rocks at between 135 and 190 million years old. It was quarried extensively in the area-one disused quarry lies opposite, behind the Fish Inn - and used to build the familiar Cotswold stone houses. The "Inferior" oolite was less satisfactory and was used in wall construction. Deep quarries were unnecessary since the stone had already been frost-riven into convenient slabs. Tilestones were found near the surface and were laid on the ground so that the frost could split them further into thin sheets.

Modern residents sometimes experience difficulty in obtaining new tiles for their repairs, since they are no longer quarried.

The shallow humps and hollows of redundant diggings make for an interesting woodland walk, signposted from the picnic area. Search closely in the thick undergrowth and you can find loose fragments of limestone and maybe even a fossil brachiopod, a prehistoric cockle once common in warm Jurassic seas.

Previous attempts to tame this knobbly landscape included a bit of hit-and-miss forestry, which explains the odd mix of larch, sycamore and beech. Only the last tree deserves to be here - the others are shamelessly out of place and shade out the pyramidal orchids and small scabious which hang on in a few place.

The walk is a short one and not especially characteristic of the Cotswolds, but valuable in that it allows almost the only free public access to the hills in the county. Children will love its unexpected twists and turns and it's great for a family game of hide-and-seek as long as you remember that the main road is unfenced.

Broadway Tower

Although Broadway Tower lies in what is described as a "Country Park", it has no connection with country parks created by HWCC under the 1968 Countryside Act. This is private land and carries a entrance charge, so it really deserves no place here. However, you can cross the scarp by public footpath to view the Avon plain. What a view it makes, too. It's easy to see why the Earl of Coventry built the elegant tower in 1799 from which to gaze over his vast estate at Croome Court. The hill is 1024 feet above sea-level and the tower is 65 feet high, so that when you stand on top, you are at the highest point in the Cotswolds. The tower was once used as an overflow library by Thomas Phillipps, the Broadway "Book King", who owned the land around the monument in the mid-19th century. His obses-

sion for collecting books and manuscripts of all kind from all parts of the globe led to connections in high society. Burne-Jones, William Morris and Rosetti stayed in the tower summerhouse and a collection of pre-Raphaelite memorabilia can be seen there today for a charge. Sir Thomas's library led eventually to heavy debts and he was forced to rob his house at nearby Middle Hill for what he could salvage. When he died, the house at Middle Hill was in terrible disrepair and fetched £120,000, a third of the value of his library which was split up and sold by his grandchildren.

Several footpaths lead downhill over the ridge-and -furrow pasture to Broadway village, a very pleasant walk at any season.

Tiddesley Wood

OSL Map 150
GR SO 929/459 (Car park)

OSP SO 84/94

On A4104 half a mile west
of Pershore. Car park on
minor road to Ramsden
west of A44.

WNCT (part private). Large
flower-rich ancient wood-
land with an extensive network of paths. Most foot-
paths flat and well-drained,
but muddy in wet weather.

Public Transport: Buses
from Worcester to Pershore.

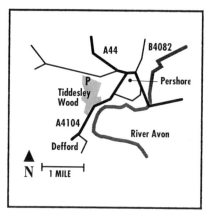

Tiddesley is a landmark wood in
every sense of the word. From
the summit of Bredon Hill it appears as a dark block rubbing
shoulders with Pershore town. On
the map it dominates the Avon
valley, a welcome wedge of green
in a chequered expanse of farmland. In the WNCT's folio of reserves it gets top billing for its
age, wildlife and beauty. Now,
thanks to the Trust, it is open to
all and should not be missed.

The most convenient access point
is to the north, along the minor
road to Ramsden. Here, beneath a
high hedge, you can park near a
stile bearing the Trust's house
martin logo. A short, gravelled
path between apple orchards

leads into the wood where there
is a map and information boards.
Woodland craft fairs and open
days are occasionally held here:
the permanent stands can be seen
throughout the year.

Exploring this large and even
wood is a delectable experience.
Try as you will to keep to the central stone-chipped ride which runs
straight through to the Avon, the
temptation to sneak along the
network of lesser paths is irresistible. So, go where you will, but
watch out for the warning flags
which indicate that the firing
range in the south-west is in use.
When the flag is hoisted, please
keep away from this section of
the wood.

With over 300 species of flower-
ing plants, Tiddesley is the richest
botanical site in the county. The
reasons for its floral diversity are

threefold: age, management and underlying soils. Recorded in the Domesday Survey of 1086, it was once common land, grazed by cattle and pigs. In 1223, the Abbot of Westminster rescinded the rights of common to empark the wood for breeding deer. This action met with profound disapproval from the tenants of the Abbot of Pershore who responded by destroying fences and hedges.

For any wood of this size to survive intact, especially on fertile soils, it needs to pay its way. From medieval times until early this century that meant providing timber and underwood. We know that in the early 19th century oaks were coppiced in Tiddesley on a 39 year cycle, useful both for their timber and tannin-rich bark. Simultaneous stands of 26 and 13 -year old oaks were grown to produce a continuous supply of wood to suit all needs. This was real forestry, a term which now seems to be restricted to conifer plantations. And, talking of conifers...

In the 1950's, the Forestry Commission rode roughshod through Tiddesley, poisoning the native coppice and replacing it with pines, Douglas fir and a few beeches. Fortunately, a lack of finances and labour meant that the underwood grew back faster than it could be controlled and many a conifer perished in the grip of a honeysuckle tourniquet. Although the planting programme was not completed, large areas of woodland became badly shaded, their native flowers repressed by the gloom. When the opportunity came for the Trust to purchase the wood, it seized it eagerly and set about removing surplus conifers and reinstating traditional coppice regimes. As a result the varying woodscapes never cease to tire.

In the first year after coppicing, plants run riot in a frantic burst of energy . Annuals appear, revelling in the sunlight and insects are attracted to the sudden flush of nectar-bearing flowers. In Tiddesley, masses of crimson marsh thistles vie for supremacy of the glades with willowherbs and, in damper runnels, purple loosestrife.A couple of years on they are gone, replaced by sprawling tangles of old man's beard, suckering aspen and hazel wands. Violets and orchids, swamped before by their coarser companions, now reach their prime. Along the rides primroses and cowslips bloom. After fifteen years they too are less in evidence, crowded out once again by the shade. It's a delicate balance and we can only wonder how these demanding plants fared in the pre-Neolithic wildwood.

Some species are rare in Worcestershire, but relatively common here. Scented agrimony, meadow saffron, and herb paris can all be found as you explore the pathways. Narrow-leaved everlasting pea is a local speciality of the lower Lias clays as is the stinking iris. In winter its vivid orange seeds linger in the frosts making this an easy plant to locate.

Tiddesley's butterfly population is spectacular. White admirals (their name is a corruption of 'admirable') glide in summer clearings and purple hairstreaks spin in the oak tops. Dragonflies are frequent too, visiting from the River Avon. In early summer look out for white-legged damselflies, pale blue and needle-thin with a white flange on each leg. So many insects attract birds aplenty, though the age of the trees limits hole-nesters.

Sparrowhawks hunt the rides by day, tawny owls by night. Nightingales breed in small numbers while warblers such as blackcaps and garden warblers are frequent in new coppice.

Your best views of mammals will probably be of introductions. Rabbits are a terrible pest in new coppice, nibbling the tender young growth. Older trees are under attack from grey squirrels, introduced in the late 19th century and irrepressible since.

Since the wood stands alone, getting lost is impossible - the central ride is never far away. If you wish for a longer walk, there is a public footpath along the banks of the Avon near the ride's junction with the A4104. This path runs for about a mile to Pershore Bridge picnic site and the town centre is conveniently close.

Sparrowhawk

138

Bredon Hill

OSL Map 150   GR Woollas
Hall SO 946/410

OSP SO 84/94 (North) GR
Westmancote SO 943/380

OSP SO 83/93 (South)

*Off minor roads from Eck-
ington and Great Comber-
ton.*

*Private. Area above West-
mancote NNR. Limestone
hill with superb views
across Worcestershire and
Gloucestershire country-
side. Largely agricultural,
but good kite flying and picnic area around. Banbury
stone. Some short and
steep sections below top.*

*Public Transport: MRW
buses 550 551 571*

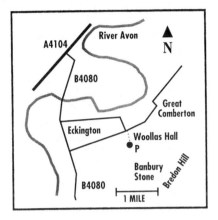

If you use the M5 motorway regularly, Bredon Hill is a familiar
sight, rising in solitary splendour
from the Avon flood-plain east of
the M50 intersection. Ringed with
a necklace of historic villages,
Bredon is a Cotswold outlier and
like those hills capped with the
honey-coloured Jurassic limestone. To stand on the summit
and take in the sweep of Worcestershire's landscape is an unforgettable experience.

On a clear day the whole county

stretches before you to the north
and west, while to the south lies
the glittering maw of the Severn
estuary. On misty autumn days
there is the fascination of watching each surrounding village revealed in turn by the unravelling
fogs. Whatever the season, Bredon will delight you as it delighted
Masefield and Housman.

However these pleasures don't
come too easily - if you want to
enjoy the views, you must walk.
There are no public roads to the
top, but compensation lies in the
host of footpaths leading from the
encircling settlements. By far the
shortest is from Woollas Hall, just
off the minor road between Great
Comberton and Eckington. Parking is limited and an early start
will secure you a space at weekends. As you climb, Woollas Hall
is revealed, an imposing house
built in 1611 by the Hanford fam-

ily. Among its treasures are a set of embroidered hangings by Lady Wyntour of Huddington, whose husband Robert perished for his involvement in the Gunpowder Plot. The path runs directly uphill, ignoring the metalled drive and heads directly for the crown of the hill.

Few wild flowers adorn the lower slopes, for these have been sprayed - the euphemism used often used even by conservationists is "improved". However there are battalions of thistles which grow here as nowhere else in the county. Most attractive are the nodding thistles with silver-green foliage and hanging magenta blooms.

Spectacular woolly-headed thistles are scattered about, their robust spines and white cottony buds making them easy to identify. Sadly, even these have been sprayed in some places and are contorted into grotesque mis-shapes.

One of the most interesting features of this part of Bredon is its collection of old and battered trees. Huge ashes, cracked and hollow with age cling to ancient field boundaries. Often their branches carry the black fungi known as King Alfred's cakes or cramp balls. Elsewhere willows hunch arthritically over spring lines where water draining through the limestone hits a bed of harder rock and is forced to the surface. Such springs extend around the entire hill and have their own special plants.

With the top now in sight, the path has faded to nothing in a landscape of dereliction. Old stone walls, rare in Worcestershire, lie in ruins all around, their boulders prised apart by the massive elders. So large are these bushes that they house breeding redstarts and are thick with Jew's ear fungus.

Everywhere the grassy hummocks are strewn with shards of golden rock, fragments of fossiliferous limestone. The commonest fossil is the shell gryphea, the devil's toe-nail, an inhabitant of the Jurassic oceans over 160 million years ago. Local quarries yield a rich harvest including sea-lilies, lamp-shells or brachiopods and cylindrical belemnites, known locally as "bullets".

Ahead now is the final struggle, a steep scarp leading to the summit. The short, but taxing climb is badly eroded, so please keep to the paths where possible. Ladies' bedstraw and lime-green cross-wort abound in the short turf, reminders of how the lower slopes used to look before conversion to sheep pasture. Butterflies suddenly appear away from pesticides; meadow browns, small skippers, gatekeepers and, best of all, marbled whites which seem to mock your ungainliness as you rest gratefully near the tower.

This unglamorous structure is known as Parson's Folly and was built in the 18th century by a Mr. Parsons of Kemerton, supposedly to raise the overall height of Bredon to exactly 1,000 feet. Just below the tower is a peculiar rock called the Banbury Stone or Elephant Stone. From certain angles it bears a remarkable resemblance to a kneeling pachyderm and is very popular with children who swarm over its knobbly surface. Legend has it that should the beast hear the chimes of Pershore Abbey far below, it will rise and lumber downhill to drink from the Avon.

Peer closely at the rocks around the tower and you will see that they are made up of tiny granules, rather like fossilised fish eggs. This is Inferior Oolite, sometimes dubbed roestone, and was formed when grains of sand were trapped in a matrix of Jurassic mud. It is "Inferior" because here it is badly weathered and of poorer quality than the classic Cotswold stone which lends distinction to so many Gloucestershire villages.

Before you to the north and west lie Housman's "coloured counties" further enlivened in recent years by the sulphur of oilseed rape and the powder-blue of flax, farmed for linseed. The Avon snakes through a mainly arable landscape which has been converted from pasture in response to EEC dairy quotas and advances in agricultural machinery. Huge open fields are now the norm, witness the hedgeless expanse behind Little Comberton. Even the surviving hedges no longer have the "Worcestershire Weed", the English elm. Once the top-heavy trees grew everywhere dark against the ripening corn. Now the ravages of Dutch Elm disease

have reduced the giants to lines of suckers. The plague is caused by a fungus which blocks the trees' water and nutrient conduction system, and is carried by the elm-bark beetles. Young elms are usually infected when about fifteen feet high and then form reservoirs of disease. The chances of seeing mature elms within our lifetimes is very small until the disease loses its virulence.

Landmarks to look out for include Pershore and its Abbey, the dark blot of Tiddesley Wood and Worcester cathedral. In the far north are the Clent Hills, obscuring the Birmingham conurbation. Closer at hand on the slopes below, are a series of hummocks and hollows, reminiscent of old quarry workings. These are caused by rainfall draining from the hard limestone summit and softening the Upper Lias rocks below. In places the liquefied layer becomes unstable and slumps downhill to be squeezed between projecting spurs of harder Middle Lias rock. At times the mud-flows travel quickly; one has been witnessed to ooze fifty feet in half an hour. The slopes above St. Catherine's Well on the west of the hill are still active and have been designated a National Nature Reserve for their geological and natural history interest.

Bredon is always much windier and cooler than the vale below, a fact worth remembering in winter when mists fill the ditches of the Iron Age hill fort. This, the only open area on the top, is privately owned, but walkers and picnickers are never turned away. Once at the summit, the choices are many. Although the plateau is intensively farmed, numerous footpaths lead around the rim and from there down to the villages of Westmancote, Overbury, Elmley Castle and Little Comberton to name but a few. Each is well worth a visit. Above Westmancote are the King and Queen Stones, between which sick children were once passed to heal them. Flower-rich bridleways criss-cross the stony arable, so that a full day's brisk walking will pass quickly by.

River Access Points

Arley SO 766/801 Riverside walk from footbridge c 4 miles south along Worcestershire Way to Bewdley. Woodland and farmland. Path through Seckley Wood, slippery in places.

Bewdley Lax Lane car park SO 789/752. Good path through fields along river bank to Stourport c 3.5 miles.

Lenchford SO 813/63 Public footpath form A4196 south of Lenchford Hotel. Short woodland walk and weir c 1 mile to Holt Fleet - return by A4133.

Grimley SO 837/607 Public footpath to river past Waggon Wheel Hotel in Grimley village. Walk of c 3 miles south to Hallow returning by footpath to Camp Lane.

Upton-on-Severn SO 854/405 Walk south through the Ham meadows continuously to Tewkesbury. Short walk returns across the Hams.

SEVERN - EAST BANK

Arley SO 766/802 Walk through Eymore Wood to Trimpley Reservoir, returning along woodland paths to Arley. Severn Valley Railway an added attraction. c 3.5 miles.

Bewdley Blackstone Picnic Site SO 795/745 Walk to Stourport for c 3.5 miles.

Stourport-on-Severn SO 808/711 From Stourport bridge through industrial landscape then fields, woods and under sandstone cliffs. Continuous path for c 7.5 miles south to Holt Fleet, where there are two riverside inns.

Holt Fleet SO 824/634 Path south for c 2.5 miles to Hawford. Return by same route necessary without detour across fields to Chatley and Sinton, or walk along A449.

Hawford SO 843/599 Short walk of c 2.5 miles south from Hawford Farm past weir to Northwick where small car park and picnic area.

Kempsey SO 847/491 South from Kempsey Ham common from church to Baynhall. Short walk of c 1.5 miles.

Uckinghall SO 868/380 Footpath from village (north of post office) to river bank and for c 1.5 miles to south.

AVON

Eckington Bridge SO 922/423 Path to Strensham Lock c 2 miles to the south. See also picnic sites for access details.

Pershore Bridge SO 952/451 Path west to Tiddesley Wood. See also picnic sites for access details.

143

Jubilee Bridge SP 001/460 Walks south to Evesham town. See also picnic sites.
Cleeve Prior SP 080/498 Walk south to Fish and Anchor near Offenham. See under Cleeve Prior.

TEME

Stanford Bridge S0 715/657 North through meadows for c 2 miles to Eardiston village.
Ham Bridge SO 737/611 North for c 2.5 miles to Shelsley Beauchamp church. Good circular walk in paths to Southwood and south via Pudford.
Bransford Bridge SO 804/532 West along south bank to Bransford c 1.5 miles.

Canal Access Points

Three canals, two still in use, thread the county. All have towpaths along which you are permitted to walk although technically these are not right of way unless they coincide with existing footpaths, and therefore may be temporarily closed by the British Waterways Board.

BIRMINGHAM & WORCESTER CANAL

Tardebigge SO 996/693 Walk from Tardebigge church along flight of 58 locks. Reservoir and pleasant cottages add to the attractions of this canal. Inn at Stoke Pound.

STAFFORDSHIRE & WORCESTERSHIRE CANAL

CAUNSALL BRIDGE - see under main text.

DROITWICH CANAL

Salwarpe SO 875/620 Walk west from Salwarpe church along river valley. Canal disused, but being partly restored. Reed-beds and salt loving plants a speciality. c 3 miles to Hawford.

Long Distance Footpaths

Footpaths are beyond the scope of this book, but three deserve special mention for their scale and their interest. All three cross areas described elsewhere and their signposts will be a temptation to any keen explorer. This is precisely the effect the Countryside Commission had in mind when it encouraged local authorities to establish long distance footpaths. These were originally called "Regional Routes", existing rights of way interwoven with permissive paths negotiated between the authorities and the landowners. Now the longest are known as National Trails and include the Pennine Way and the Coast to Coast Path.

Worcestershire's walks are humbler but no less interesting, taking in superb countryside and are the best way of getting to know the county in depth. Two, the Worcestershire Way and the North Worcestershire Path, have been developed by HWCS, while the Wychavon Way was created by Wychavon District Council. They can easily be walked in two or three days or tackled in segments. Carefully devised loop-walks allow you to explore what the Countryside Commission calls the "wider countryside" and return to your starting point, thus avoiding the familiar bane of all long-distance walkers - having to take two vehicles!

The Worcestershire Way:
Northern end - Kingsford Country Park. OSL Map 138 GR SO 829/822
Southern end - Cowleigh Park, Malvern. OSL Map 150 GR SO 766/475

This 39-mile walk was declared open in 1989. It runs along the western fringe of Worcestershire and takes in some of the very best views in the county. Fit walkers do it in two days, but a leisurely three-day saunter will allow you to sample the excellent pubs en route and revel in the scenery. You can walk the entire length without a map by following the waymarked arrows (blue on bridleways, yellow on footpaths), but HWCS produce a detailed map-pack which will add to your appreciation.

With a little planning you can avoid using a car. The most convenient route is from the southern end, where Cowleigh Park is just over a mile from Malvern Link railway station. From the start, the Way heads north through fields and alongside woods to cross the A4103 at Storridge. It climbs the slopes of Birchwood Common, where Elgar composed the music to The Dream of Gerontius, and descends to Longley Green, where the Nelson Inn makes a pleasant stopover.

From here the route switchbacks across the limestone ridge of the Suckley

Hills where spruce and fir are usurping the limes and wild service trees. Oast houses and timber-framed dwellings mark one of the county's oldest landscapes as far as Knightsford Gap where the path crosses the A44 and the River Teme. For northward walkers Ankerdine Hill is a formidable obstacle, the steepest main road in Worcestershire. After pausing for breath at the summit picnic site, follow the path as it kinks eastward into the folds of Nipple Coppice to re-emerge on the main road at Berrow Green, south of Martley. From here there's a plunge to the banks of the Teme at Kingswood Common.

Your acquaintance with the river is brief, however, for soon comes the climb onto Rodge Hill, possibly the finest section of the Way. Now you can enjoy three miles of uninterrupted ridgetop walking with magnificent views across the Teme valley below. Rodge Hill gives way to Walsgrave Hill and Walsgrave to Abberley where the elegant clock-tower becomes a half-way marker. Those wanting refreshment will not be disappointed by the Manor Arms in Abberley village where you can contemplate the wooded slopes of Abberley Hill, your next target.

The route leaves the hill to strike north across the modern prairies of Heightington. Arable land is not always restored for walkers as quickly as it might be and boots are essential if you want to avoid platforms of caked mud. The going is gentle across country to Bewdley with its wealth of hotels and eating places. You leave the town along the Severnside path to Arley where it crosses a footbridge and twists cunningly uphill into Eymore Wood. Emerging near the A 442 at Shatterford, you are on the final stretch, a downhill stroll across pasture to Kingsford, with a last struggle to the top of the Kinver Edge.

Here, if you have the energy, are the beginnings of the Staffordshire Way (92 miles) and North Worcestershire Path. A short walk into Kinver village allows you to join the public transport system. Buses run regularly into Stourbridge town three miles away.

Further information; Leaflet and map-pack available from HWCS.

The North Worcestershire Path:
Western end: Kingsford Country Park. OSL Map 138. GR SO 829/822
Eastern end: Major's Green OSL Map 139. GR SP 101/782

If the Worcestershire Way is almost exclusively rural, the North Worcestershire Path is contrastingly suburban. Throughout its 27 mile length you are never far from the West Midlands conurbation, but can still explore a varied and beautiful stretch of countryside. Its route is a triumph of planning, here flirting dangerously with county boundaries, there succumbing briefly to the pull of a housing estate, but amazingly, never losing its appeal.

Throughout its length the path is well marked by arrows and, since 1991, has been extended by the HWCC Urban Fringe Countryside Action Project to reach into Worcestershire's far north-eastern corner at Major's Green, near Shirley. There is little parking space at this eastern end, though the landlord of the Drawbridge at Major's Green will oblige, especially if you treat yourself to a celebratory drink on completion (or to help you get off the starting-block!)

At Kingsford, there are no such problems. From the conifer groves, the Way strikes eastwards across sandy farmland to cross the River Stour at Caunsall. Flattish walking takes you to Hagley where the route is threatened by the proposed Southern Orbital M42 extension. Enjoy the attractive countryside around Churchill and Stakenbridge; the area is due to be blitzed by a massive intersection planned for completion in 1997, unless a minor miracle intervenes.

At Hagley the Way is lightly embroiled in a housing estate, before crossing the A456 and skirting the grounds of Hagley Hall. Soon you begin to climb up onto the Clent Hills, past the Four Stones, across the saddle at High Harcourt Farm and the top of Walton Hill, the county's second highest point. The next stretch is a little more taxing, dipping into Shutmill valley, then climbing steeply to Romsley Hill. Near at hand across the M5 bridge is Waseley hills Country Park with magnificent views across southern Birmingham. The city is never closer here as you clip the edge of Rubery and ascend the bosky slopes of the Lickey Hills. Your descent from Lickey leads past the Austin Rover works at Cofton and around the shore of Upper Bittell Reservoir with its wildlife and sailing-boats. From here the going is less hilly through a patchwork of small fields and copses until you reach Forhill Picnic Site and the Peacock Inn. The final stretch across the agricultural plain may surprise you by being in Worcestershire at all - it's still unexplored and isolated in spite of its proximity to Birmingham. There is only one urban encounter, a small but unavoidable trudge through the streets of Hollywood (yes, really!) before you complete the path in a marshy pasture at Major's Green

Further information: Free path leaflet from HWCS.

Loopwalk leaflets: The Icknield Ways and three cycle routes, from the Urban Fringe Countryside Action Project, Planning Dept. County Hall, Worcester.

The Wychavon Way:
Northern end: Holt Fleet bridge. OSL Map 150. GR SO 824/633
Southern end: Winchcombe. OSL Map 150. GR SP 026/283

Wychavon District Council have developed this 40-mile footpath which is particularly welcome since it allows you to explore areas of agricultural

Worcestershire otherwise devoid of access points. It is waymarked through-out its length by yellow Wychavon symbols and arrows, blue for bridle-ways, yellow for footpaths and white on roads. One useful feature of the walk is that you only need to carry one map, O/S sheet 150.

From Holt Fleet, on the River Severn, the route crosses the parkland of Ombersley House to the village of Hadley. Beyond the Hadley Brook, you are in the grounds of Westwood House, once the site of a Benedictine nunnery. The impressive house has now been converted into private flats. After reaching the farmland of Crutch Hill, the route swings south into Droitwich town, famous since Roman times for its salt deposits. Salt mined here was transported along the Roman road to Hanbury and far beyond to satisfy the invaders' savoury tastes. Between Droitwich and Flyford Flavell, the Way enters one of its more anonymous sections, punctuated by the settlements of Shernal Green and Earl's Common and a motley of ancient coppice.

At Flyford Flavell, you cross the A422 to enter the sweeping agricultural landscapes of Abberton and the Lenches. "Lench" is a variant of linck or lynchet, a steep slope ploughed horizontally to prevent land-slippage. At Cropthorne, there are hints of Evesham Vale in the fruit orchards. The Way crosses the Avon here and slogs for over two miles over farmland be-fore it climbs the eastern slopes of Bredon Hill. Your reward for getting this far is a superb panorama of southern Worcestershire and the frontier hills of the Cotswolds.

After a gradual descent from Bredon, the path leaves the county south of the A435 near Ashton-under-Hill. Its end lies some five miles distant at Winchcombe village, beyond the limestone hummocks of Dumbleton and Alderton Hills.

Further information: Map leaflet with tourist information from Leisure and Tourism Information Services,Wychavon District Council, Pershore.

Picnic Sites

Most of the sites described in this book are ideal picnic places but there are a number of additional picnic sites scattered throughout Worcestershire. The list below describes those provided by Hereford and Worcestershire Countryside Service. All have picnic tables and information and many have circular walks leading from them. For further information about any of the sites, contact Hereford and Worcester Countryside Service at County Hall, Worcester.

Ankerdine Hill Picnic Place: See account on page 68

Avoncroft Museum: OSL Map 150 GR S0 954/684
South of Bromsgrove on the A4024. Picnic site adjoins the Avoncroft Museum of buildings, a magnificent collection of restored and reconstructed Worcestershire architecture.

Blackstone Picnic Place: OSL Map 138 GR SO 796/743
South of Bewdley on the B4195. Riverside site with pleasant walking along the Severn Valley south to Stourport-on-Severn.

Cleeve Prior: See account on page 130

Eckington Bridge: OSL Map 150 GR SO 923/422
On B4080 2 miles south-west of Pershore. Riverside site with walks along south bank of Avon to Strensham and west to Birlingham and Nafford.

Fish Hill Picnic Place: See account on page 134

Forhill Picnic Place: OSL Map 139 GR SP 055/757
On minor roads between King's Norton and the M42. Ryknield Street, an Old Roman Road runs immediately west of the site. Good access point for the North Worcestershire Path.

Jubilee Bridge Picnic Place: OSL Map 150 GR SP 00l/457
Riverside picnics and walks in the Cropthorne and Fladbury areas. The Wychavon Way crosses the Avon here on the minor road which joins the two villages.

Pershore Bridge: OSL Map 150 GR S0 954/451
Riverside picnic site with walks west along north track of the Avon.

Twyford Farm: OSL Map 150 GR SP 045/465
East of A435, one mile north of Evesham. Orchards and riverside walks along the Avon into Evesham town, observation tower and craft centre.

Tourist Information Centres

There is no doubt that your first port-of-call in a new area should be the nearest Tourist Information Centre. All the information you will need about places to visit, local accommodation, facilities and current events is on hand, together with a full range of publications. Centres are divided into two categories and Grade One Centres are open throughout the year while Grade Two centres are open seasonally - the latter are marked with an asterisk below. All are well-marked with Information signs for both pedestrians and motorists.

Bewdley: St George's Hall, Load Street, Bewdley DY12 2EQ
Tel: (0299) 404740

Broadway*: 1 Cotswold Court, Broadway, WR12 7AA
Tel: (0386) 852937

Bromsgrove: 47–49 Worcester Rd, Bromsgrove B61 7DN
Tel: (0527) 31809

Droitwich: St Richard's House, Victoria Square, Droitwich WR9 8DS
Tel: (0905) 774312

Evesham: Almonry Museum, Abbey Gate, Evesham WR11 4BG
Tel: (0562) 829400

Kidderminster*:
Severn Valley Railway Station, Comberton Hill, Kidderminster DY10 1QX
Tel: (0386) 446944

Malvern: Winter Gardens Complex, Grange Road, Malvern WR14 3HB
Tel: (0684) 892289

Pershore: 19 High Street, Pershore WR10 1AA
Tel: (0386) 554262

Redditch: Civic Square, Alcester Street, Redditch B98 8AH
Tel: (0527)60806

Upton-on-Severn*:
The Pepperpot, Church Street, Upton-on-Severn WR8 0HT
Tel: (06846) 4200

Worcester: The Guildhall, High Street, Worcester WR1 2EY
Tel: (0905) 726311/723471

Ramblers Association

The Ramblers' Association exists to pursue four main aims: to promote rambling, to protect footpaths, to seek public access to open country and to defend the natural beauty of the countryside. Set up in 1935, the association has a large membership and more than 330 local RA groups. Members receive copies of the association's quarterly colour magazine and our annual Rambler's Yearbook and Accommodation Guide. In addition, they may borrow OS maps from our extensive library and are eligible for discounts in certain outdoor equipment stores.

Local groups organise regular programmes of walks as well as practical footpath work and social evenings. To campaign with even greater success, we need to increase our membership so that we are seen to be truly representative of all those who love rambling in the countryside.

For more information, please contact:
The Ramblers' Association,
1–5 Wandsworth Road,
London SW8 2XX.
Telephone: 071 582 6878.

Open Spaces Society

The Open Spaces Society, formally the Commons, Open Spaces and Footpaths Preservation Society, was founded in 1865 and is Britain's oldest national conservation body. We campaign to protect common land, village greens, open spaces and public paths and your right to enjoy them. We advise local authorities and the public on common land and public path law, and give support to campaigns on a local level.

Members have instant access to the society's advisory service; receive the society's informative journal three times a year and are entitled to discount on the society's publications. For more information please contact:
The Open Spaces Society,
25a Bell Street,
Henley on Thames,
Oxon RG9 2BA.
Telephone: (0491) 573535.
(Registered charity no. 214753).

THE OPEN SPACES SOCIETY

The Worcestershire Nature Conservation Trust

The Worcestershire Nature Conservation Trust has 60 wildlife reserves covering 1,500 acres of Worcestershire. Many of these are open to the public for the quiet enjoyment of nature and the countryside. The wide variety of woods, marshes, heaths and meadows are amongst the finest of their type in the county.

Anyone can join the Trust. If you do so you will be helping to save our County's heritage. Much has been destroyed in the last fifty years. It is very important to conserve what is left. If you become a member of the Trust your subscription will help stem the tide of destruction. As a member you will receive details of the reserves and special mailings from the Trust.

Worcestershire Nature Conservation Trust, Lower Smite Farm, Smite Hill, Hindlip, Worcester WR3 8SZ. Tel: 0905 754919.

C HEREFORD AND WORCESTER COUNTY
C_OUNTRYSIDE SERVICE_

Hereford and Worcester Countryside Service looks after some of the largest areas

open to the public in Worcestershire, Clent Hills Country Park for instance - and

some of the smallest too!. The Countryside Service is part of the County Council,

but it manages much property for other owners in order that the public may use

and enjoy it. Management must also preserve the natural environment from the

effects of neglect and overuse. Local Nature Reserves and Sites of Special

Scientific Interest such as Hartlebury Common demand extra care.

Small picnic places are being provided. They make a starting point of walks,

whether local, like Eckington Wharf with its riverside walks along the Avon, or

longer distance, like Cowleigh Park and Ankerdine Common on the Worcestershire

Way.

The Countryside Service is helped by volunteers in its work. If you might be

interested in helping too, or for further information, please ring 0905 766493 for

the south of the county or 0562 710025 for the north.

COUNTRY PARKS

Clent Hills Country Park
Tree-clad hills with magnificent views. Two easy access trails.
500acres. Off A453 Birmingham and Kidderminster road. North area

Kingsford Country Park
Pinewoods and open heath near Kinver Edge. The start of three
medium distance paths. 200acres. North of Kidderminster between
Kinver and Wolverley. North Area.

Leapgate Country Park
Open Heathland. Hartlebury Common with Hillditch pool and
coppice is an important Local Nature Reserve. Level walking and
riding on the disused railway line from Stourport to Hartlebury.
250 acres. Just south of Stourport on B4193 to Hartlebury.
South area.

Waseley Hills Country Park
Grass covered hills with spectacular views, small woods and ponds.
Visitor Centre with café. 150 acres. South of Rubery near
Birmingham and Exit 4 of M5. North area.

Worcester Woods Country Park
Ancient woodlands with walks and orienteering course.
Countryside Centre with café and events field. 140 acres. East of
Worcester near County Hall off A422. South area.

PICNIC PLACES

ANKERDINE COMMON *South area. G.R. 736566. On*
Worcestershire Way. Off B4197 between Knightwick and Martley.
AVONCROFT *North area. G.R. 954685. At Avoncroft Museum of*
Buildings. Off A38 south east of Bromsgrove.
BLACKSTONE *South area. G.R. 796743. Near Worcestershire Way. At*
junction of B4195 to Stourport and Bewdley Bypass.
CLEEVE PRIOR *South area. G.R. 079496. By River Avon 0.5 miles*
west of Cleeve Prior Church down Mill Lane.
COWLEIGH PARK *South area . G.R. 766476. End of Worcestershire*
Way on B4219 between Malvern and Storridge.
ECKINGTON WHARF *South area. G.R. 923422. By River Avon. On*
B4080 between Pershore and Tewkesbury 0.5 mile N. of Eckington.
FISH HILL *South area. G.R. 120370. On Cotswold Way. On A44*
Evesham to Moreton in Marsh 2 miles E. of Broadway.
FORHILL *North area. G.R. 056755. On N. Worcestershire Path. On*
minor road Redditch to Kings Norton, 1 mile W. of Wythall.
JUBILEE BRIDGE *South area. G.R. 001456. By River Avon 3 miles*
west of Evesham on minor road Fladbury to Cropthorne.
PERSHORE BRIDGE *South area. G.R. 952451. On River Avon. On*
A44 0.25 miles east of Pershore.
TWYFORD FARM *South area. G.R. 045466. Next to Twyford Farm*
Park. Off A436 1.5 miles north of Evesham.

Supported by

COUNTRYSIDE
COMMISSION

To Jo, John, Len and Malcolm
with thanks for a wonderful Worcestershire Way weekend.

About the Author

Brett Westwood is one of those rare and fortunate individuals whose professional and personal interests have been energetically focussed into a
committed vocation. Until recently he was Interpretation Officer for Hereford & Worcester Countryside Service; currently he is Tourism and Mar-
keting Officer for a local authority.

His previous publications include the text of "The Wye Valley Walk" and
contributing to "The Worcestershire Way" map pack. He feels justifiably
proud of his co-authorship, with Harry Green, of the best-selling "The Nature of Worcestershire", which has become a standard work of reference,
to which he also contributed his excellent illustrations. Brett's illustrations
may also be found in "The Birds of the West Midlands", "The Bird-
watcher's Yearbook", "Rabbits" and "Mice" (Shire), British Birds magazine
and the West Midland Bird Club annual reports. He is also a co-ordinator
for a floral atlas of Worcester, is involved in mapping schemes for dragonflies, reptiles and amphibians, both in preparation, and is a member of the
Botanical Society of The British Isles, and Worcestershire Nature Conservation Trust.